ARCHITECTURE + automobiles

ARCHITECTURE + *automobiles*

by Philip Jodidio

images
Publishing

Published in Australia in 2011 by
The Images Publishing Group Pty Ltd
ABN 89 059 734 431
6 Bastow Place, Mulgrave, Victoria 3170, Australia
Tel: +61 3 9561 5544 Fax: +61 3 9561 4860
books@imagespublishing.com
www.imagespublishing.com

National Library of Australia Cataloguing-in-Publication entry:

Author: Jodidio, Philip
Title: Architecture and automobiles / by Philip Jodidio.
ISBN: 9781864703306 (hbk.)
Notes: Includes index.
Subjects: Architecture.
               Architectural design – Influence
               Automobiles – Design and construction.
               Automobiles – Design and construction –
                 Influence.

Dewey Number: 725

Coordinating editor: Beth Browne

Production by The Graphic Image Studio Pty Ltd,
Mulgrave, Australia
www.tgis.com.au

Pre-publishing services by United Graphic Pte Ltd, Singapore

Printed on 140 gsm GoldEast Matt Art paper by Everbest
Printing Co. Ltd., in Hong Kong/China

IMAGES has included on its website a page for special notices
in relation to this and its other publications. Please visit
www.imagespublishing.com.

Contents

Enriched by the Beauty of Speed

We declare that the splendor of the world has been enriched by a new beauty: the beauty of speed. A racing automobile with its bonnet adorned with great tubes like serpents with explosive breath … a roaring motor car which seems to run on machine-gun fire, is more beautiful than the Victory of Samothrace.

The Futurist Manifesto
F. T. Marinetti, 1909

In a sense, the history of 20th- and 21st-century architecture is most intimately linked to the automobile, to a new vision of space and time, perhaps first articulated by *The Futurist Manifesto* in 1909. When the automobile was new and space was still to be conquered, architecture itself could no longer be static. For the Futurists, the Lingotto factory in Turin by Giacomo Matte-Trucco (1869–1934) was the 'first built invention of Futurism'. With its rooftop test track and great spiralling internal ramps, it was an ode to movement and the new modernity, in spite of its weighty reinforced-concrete presence. That Fiat and the Agnelli family asked Renzo Piano to renovate or perhaps reinvent Lingotto is a testimony to its enduring significance as a work of modern architecture. Here, the automobile and the building first became one.

America, with its endless roads and corresponding wanderlust, may be the place where automobiles and architecture found true unity. More than roadside diners and service stations, the American love affair with the car is at the origin of the quintessential motor city, Los Angeles, where pedestrians are anathema. Robert Venturi paid homage to the architecture of movement and commerce in his seminal book *Learning from Las Vegas* (Massachusetts Institute of Technology, 1972): 'The parking lot is the parterre of the asphalt landscape … But it is the highway signs, through their sculptural forms or pictorial silhouettes, their particular positions in space, their inflected shapes, and their graphic meanings that identify and unify the megatexture.'

It was not until the 1970s and the shock of rising oil prices that the ubiquity of the automobile began to be tainted with the spectre of its limits. Architects like James Wines and his SITE group from New York dared to bury old cars beneath a sheet of asphalt like a black burial cloth. The group Ant Farm created the celebrated *Cadillac Ranch*, a public art installation and sculpture in Amarillo, Texas in 1974 – its cars half buried in the earth, nose first, inclined at an angle corresponding to that of the Great Pyramid of Giza in Egypt. But these funerary works surely did not mark the end of the culture of the automobile, only the end of what the French call its insouciance, its carefree youth. Feats of engineering and architecture like Norman Foster's Millau Bridge in southern France were still to come, just as parking lots as far as the eye can see encircle and define so much urban space.

This book does not seek to recount the history of the relationship between the automobile and architecture, but rather to put a spotlight on a certain number of examples, ranging from Renzo Piano at Lingotto on to more recent examples of how the car influences and shapes architecture. The first decade of the 21st century saw automobile manufacturers including Mercedes Benz, Porsche and Volkswagen build museums or even entire complexes dedicated to their products, seen practically as works of art. Although the economic crisis unleashed in 2008 will surely reduce the number of such extravagant buildings in the near future, it would appear that cars have come to be venerated almost as much as works of art, and that their museums now begin to rival those dedicated to Rembrandt or Picasso (indeed, the French manufacturer Citroën has not hesitated to name one of its models after the Spanish painter). As a utilitarian object bound by strict rules of manufacturing and cost, the car has often fascinated architects, from Le Corbusier to Buckminster Fuller, to Zaha Hadid, whose Z-Car is one of the projects featured in this volume.

While the American highway celebrated the culture of movement and commerce, an idea still explored by architects like Elliott Associates and Kanner Architects in the United States, much of the architecture related to the automobile today could be termed more subtle, or set at a certain remove from the unbridled love of the road that formed so much of the United States. The masterful Swiss architect Mario Botta and the talented Dutch group ONL have designed acoustic barriers along highways in their respective countries – countering the noise generated by busy roads, rather than just glorifying the automobile. Young Paris-based architects Jakob + MacFarlane reused an abandoned automobile plant on the outskirts of Paris as the new communications centre for Renault. In this instance, it is the dead or empty space generated by automobiles that the architects were called on to bring back to life.

This is not to say that the glamour of speed and sculptural design in cars is forgotten – indeed car racing, especially at its highest level, has recently seen a number of intriguing race course designs created by talented architects such as those at Populous. Then too, the most prestigious automobile brands, from Rolls Royce to McLaren and Ferrari have called on such architects as Nicholas Grimshaw, Norman Foster and Masimilliano Fuksas to create research or sales facilities that prove there is still much to be said in the ongoing relationship between cars and architecture.

Factors such as high gasoline prices or the fear of pollution have taken their toll on the euphoric dreams of the Futurists and even the road culture of America, but there is in the movement of the automobile, and the great attention often paid to its design, a constant and renewed link to the form and function of contemporary architecture. The few examples published here are something like the tip of the iceberg, an indication that cars and buildings will always have a creative rapport. The grand Mercedes Benz Museum in Stuttgart by UNStudio is a temple dedicated to the car. The architecture of our time will surely continue to be 'enriched by the beauty of speed'.

Philip Jodidio

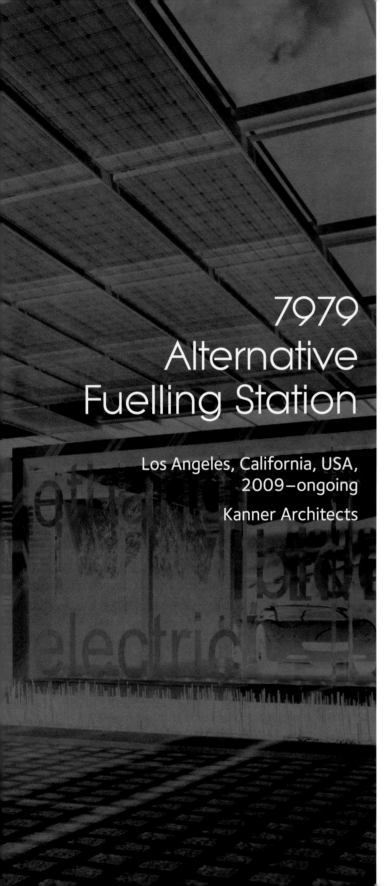

7979
Alternative
Fuelling Station

Los Angeles, California, USA,
2009–ongoing

Kanner Architects

This design proposal is for the first alternative fuelling station, showroom and store in a city dominated by the automobile – Los Angeles. Rather than petroleum, this station offers pumps for biodiesel, ethanol and hydrogen as well as electric fuelling ports. The roof and south-facing wall of the 279-square-metre structure are covered with photovoltaic panels that will be capable of returning ample power to the city grid. Sustainable crops such as corn and sugar cane will be featured in the landscaping.

The hyper-horizontal modernist building design is constructed of recycled steel. The interior of the showroom and store is sheltered by a dual-layered glass system that keeps it cool inside on warm days and warm on cool days. In-floor radiant heated coils supplied by solar-heated water provide heating. Almost all materials – inside and out – are recycled. The exterior paving will be permeable. And with no petroleum on site, all absorbed water will be clean and environmentally safe.

1 *The showroom is fully glazed, allowing vehicles to be seen from the exterior*

2 *The emphasis on the simplicity of the architecture corresponds to its ecological credentials*

1

2

1 Store
2 Showroom
3 Information counter
4 Video display area
5 Storage area
6 Restroom
7 Turf block ground cover
8 Electric charging station
9 Ethanol dispensers
10 Driveway entry
11 Photovoltaic wall
12 Information wall
13 Auto display platform
14 Billboard wall

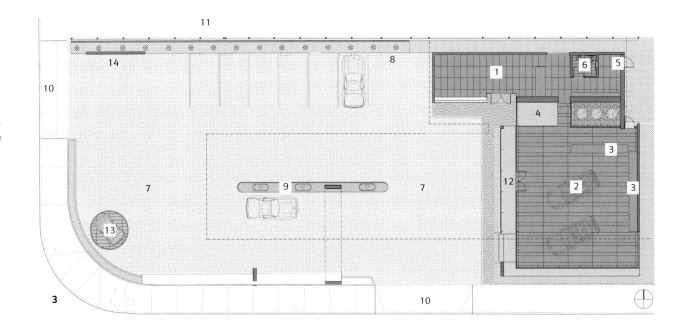

3 *A plan of the entire station emphasises straight lines and geometric design*   **4** *Photovoltaic panels are inserted into the canopy visible below*
5 *The specific nature of the station is signalled through signage and poster space*   **6** *The horizontal, open lines of the architecture make the advertisements and vehicles highly visible*

4

5

6

Acoustic Barrier

Chiasso, Switzerland, 1993–2003

Mario Botta

This noise protection structure was designed ten years before it was built on the N2 Motorway between Chiasso and Mendrisio in Switzerland. The barrier is situated in the municipalities of Chiasso, Balerna, Vacallo and Morbio Inferiore. Mario Botta worked on this project with acoustics specialists Eng. Bonalumi and Ferrari SA (Giubiasco).

The barrier has a continuous reinforced concrete plinth, tree structure, round steel sections and plates of clear soundproof laminated safety glass, as well as sound-absorbent panels covered in lacquered perforated aluminium sheeting. The curving, open nature of the design makes the barrier less oppressive than many such roadside structures, while achieving the noise abatement goals as intended.

1 *Tree-like columns support the structure's sweeping roof, combining aesthetic and practical features*

1

2 *The architecture allows for generous views of the sky despite enclosing the noisy highway*   **3** *A section drawing shows the larger arching roof that spans the Viale Galli and only partially covers the highway*   **4** *The Viale Galli is to the right, and the highway to the left*   **5** *Residential buildings are located very close to the barrier*

2

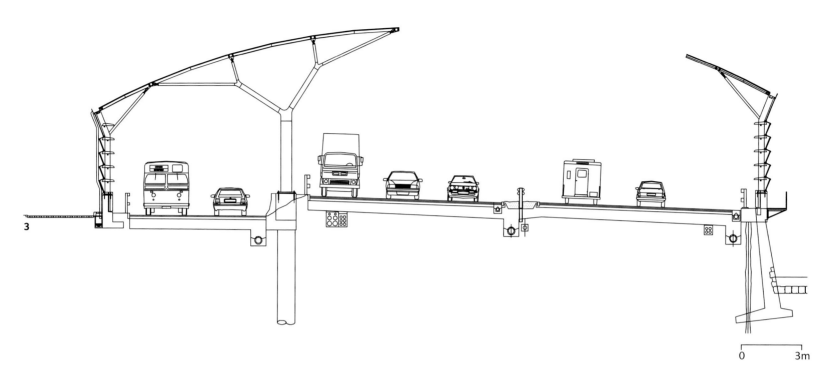

3

4

5

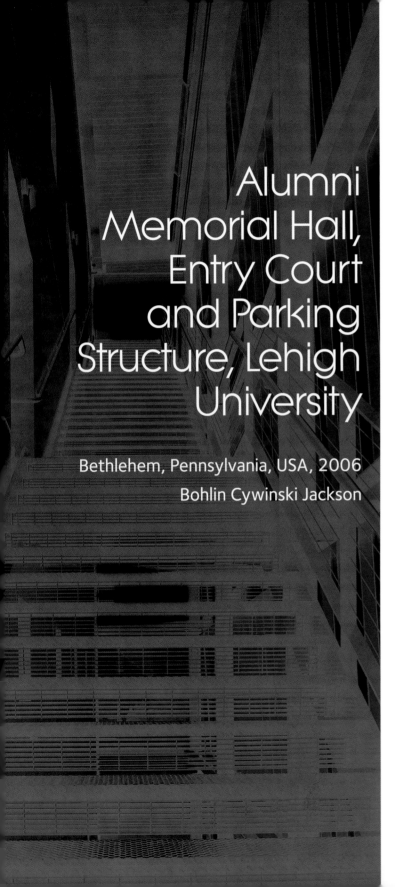

Alumni Memorial Hall, Entry Court and Parking Structure, Lehigh University

Bethlehem, Pennsylvania, USA, 2006

Bohlin Cywinski Jackson

This 2045-square-metre structure provides parking for 330 cars. Alumni Memorial Hall is Lehigh University's principal campus gateway and had been faced by a surface parking lot. The architects relocated a campus observatory that had been surrounded by the existing parking lot and in its place built a precast concrete parking structure that is partially concealed in a steep hillside.

The overall goal of the architecture is to allow it to assume a sculptural quality in order to disguise its utilitarian role. To this end, its north face is covered with shingled layers of fritted glass. The placement of the new garage to the south of Alumni Memorial Hall allowed the architects to create a generous entry court with pedestrian access, car drop off and the garage entrance in front of the building, with a walled garden and stone and water feature.

1 *Visitors arrive in a landscaped forecourt to Alumni Hall before entering the garage beyond*

1

2

3

2 *The inventive structural system more than doubles access to light and views* **3** *The overall aesthetic treatment is intrinsic to the structural system*

4 *The multilayered procession from courtyard to garage transforms the ritual of parking*

ALUMNI MEMORIAL HALL, ENTRY COURT AND PARKING STRUCTURE, LEHIGH UNIVERSITY 21

5

5 *In the evening, the delicately detailed glass wall of the stair becomes an elegant backlit screen to the arrival court below*

6 *The inner courtyard is planted with large caliper maple trees*   **7** *Detail showing king post truss above the vehicle entry*

6

7

Audi Forum Museum Mobile

Ingolstadt, Germany, 2000

Henn Architekten

This 9600-square-metre structure is located on the Ingolstadt Audi factory premises, which were more or less closed to the public for many years. The architects worked in close collaboration with the building owners to create a distinct architectural language.

The building's transparency makes internal flows visible from outside. The brand's identity is symbolised in the building's language and thus open to the public. The Museum Mobile is a three-dimensional content hub and the fulcrum of the Audi Forum's building ensemble. In regard to town planning it formulates the entrance to the works site, and in terms of visual content it embodies transparency and mobility.

The circular façades and exhibition space of the building contribute to the impression of mobility that was sought by both the client and the architects, while generous glazing achieves the element of transparency.

Opposite *Few elements, other than the vehicle parked in front of the entrance, give a hint of the function of the Audi Forum*

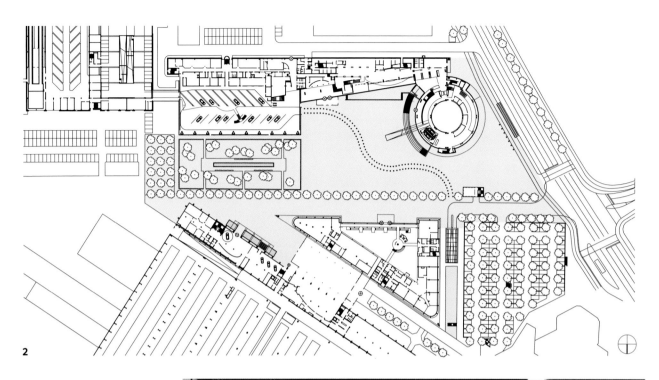

2

3

4

5

6

7

2 A site plan shows the round volume of the entrance pavilion   **3** The rather complex geometry of the interior allows for views through spaces   **4** The history of Audi vehicles is presented on these curved, open ramps, visible from other points in the building   **5** The open central atrium with exhibition platforms arranged around the main skylight   **6** An exterior view that emphasises the continuity between interior and exterior design **7** A curving ramp leads visitors into the exhibition spaces

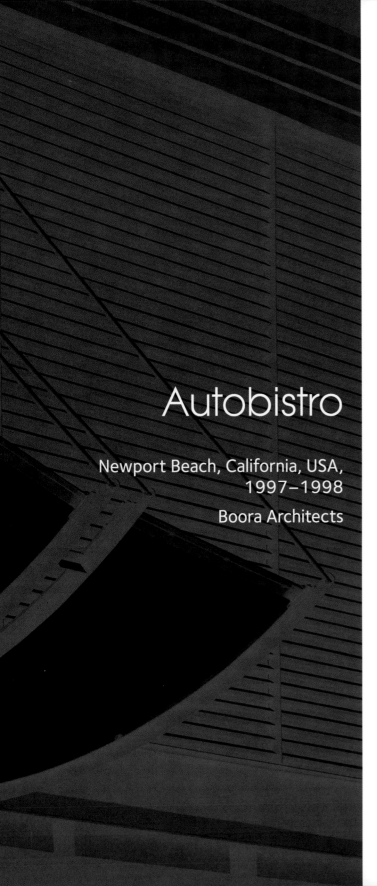

Autobistro

Newport Beach, California, USA,
1997–1998
Boora Architects

United States highways, from the iconic Route 66 to many lesser arteries, have long been the location for unexpected architecture. Service stations, roadside restaurants and motels have all been the object of careful study, particularly those in California. This project represents a new take on the genre. The architects describe it as 'a quick-service restaurant featuring healthy haute cuisine and specialty drinks to go'.

Located on the Pacific Coast Highway, the 120-square-metre building has an elevated kitchen that allows 'drive-under' traffic, but the architects clearly meant to go beyond standard designs in other ways as well. The Autobistro is a commercial building, but its eye-catching form and blue colour has made it a form of public art, a local landmark and a commercial icon, proving that roadside architecture in the US is far from dead.

Opposite *With its elevated form and colour, the Autobistro stands out from the more 'kitsch' of Los Angeles automobile culture*

2

3

2 *Graphics, such as the neon sign at the corner of the structure, call further attention to the unusual configuration* **3** *Seen at night, the building calls on the typology of the service station, but elevates the genre for another purpose* **Opposite** *Set against a foreground of cars and more traditional architecture, the Autobistro makes for a unique presence in a city of automobiles*

Automotive Complex for GCC

Abu Dhabi, United Arab Emirates,
2005–ongoing
ONL

This master plan for an automobile-related complex was conceived around a 2.5-kilometre-long terminal building with satellite structures for the showrooms, garages and retail premises of various car brands. The complex covers more than 6 square kilometres. Test driving tracks are of course part of the design, but so too are a hotel, conference centre, a car museum, design academy and a children's car track. The Automotive Complex's core business is to offer a high level of service to car customers and, as the architects suggest, 'an appealing attraction for families with children and ... must-see shows and demos for people with a specific interest in new technical developments and in the styling and design of cars'.

The architects have chosen two themes – speed and friction – as the guiding concepts of the complex. As they explain, 'Everyone likes to go fast, but reality balances out the speed because of the friction'. As is usually the case with its computer-driven concepts, ONL's Automotive Complex for GCC has contributed to the emergence of new architectural forms – in this instance forms specifically related to the automobile.

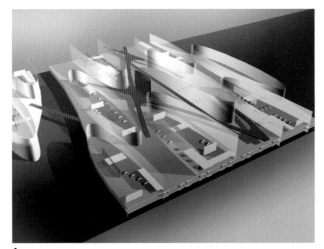

1

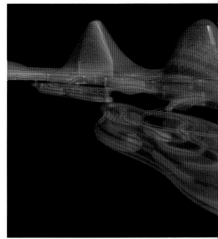

2

1 *Axonometric showing how interior spaces flow into each other, in much the same way as the exterior façades*   **2** *The futuristic external lines of the complex are related to sand dunes*
3 *Interior car display spaces and the hotel entrance assume a more conventional appearance*   **4** *Exterior surfaces give an impression of movement and can be used to advertise certain brands*
5 *The facility combines not only tracks and sales areas, but also a hotel, making it a resort destination*

3

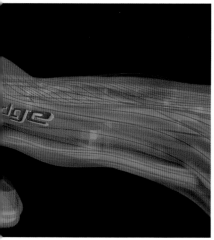

4

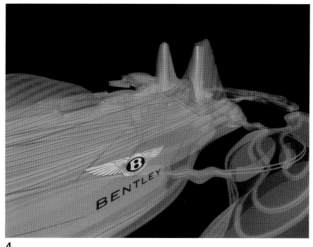

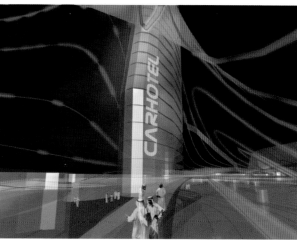

5

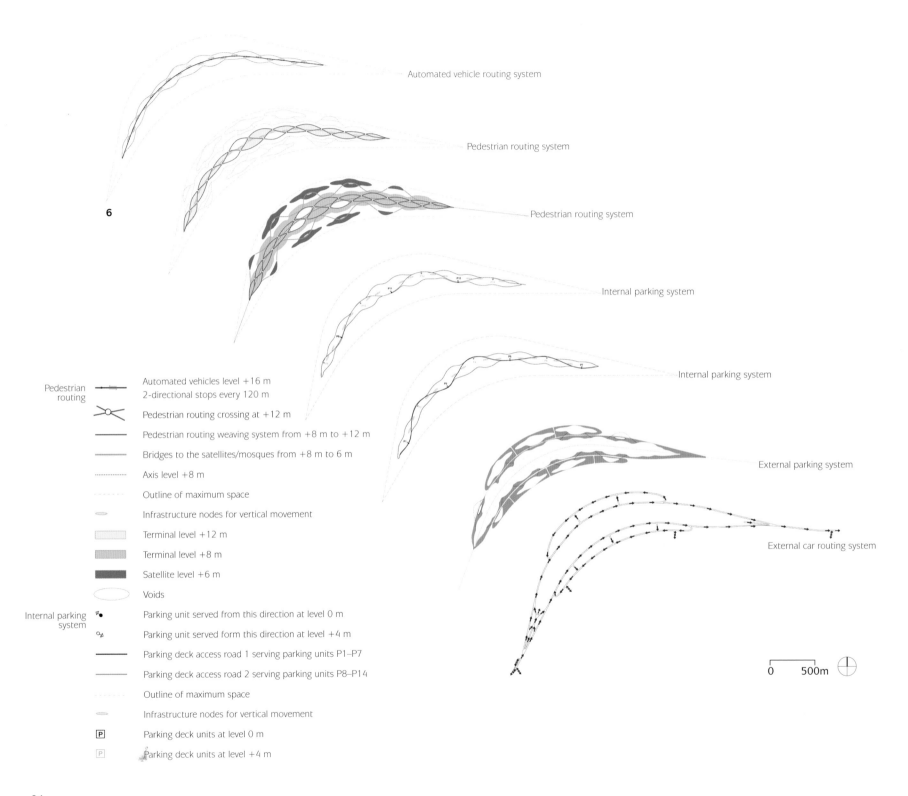

Automated vehicle routing system

Pedestrian routing system

Pedestrian routing system

Internal parking system

Internal parking system

External parking system

External car routing system

Pedestrian routing

Automated vehicles level +16 m
2-directional stops every 120 m

Pedestrian routing crossing at +12 m

Pedestrian routing weaving system from +8 m to +12 m

Bridges to the satellites/mosques from +8 m to 6 m

Axis level +8 m

Outline of maximum space

Infrastructure nodes for vertical movement

Terminal level +12 m

Terminal level +8 m

Satellite level +6 m

Voids

Internal parking system

Parking unit served from this direction at level 0 m

Parking unit served form this direction at level +4 m

Parking deck access road 1 serving parking units P1–P7

Parking deck access road 2 serving parking units P8–P14

Outline of maximum space

Infrastructure nodes for vertical movement

P Parking deck units at level 0 m

P Parking deck units at level +4 m

6

0   500m

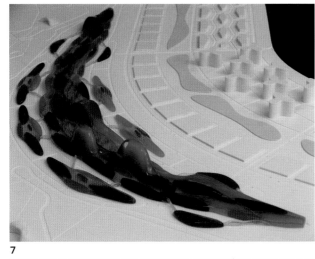

7

8

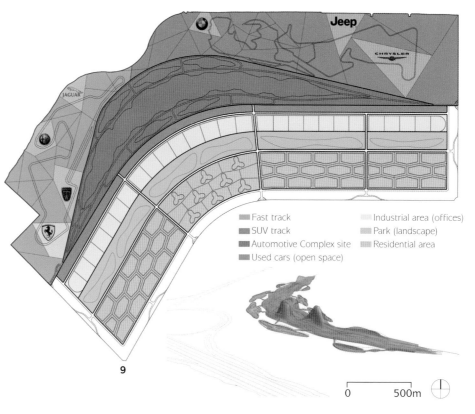

Fast track
SUV track
Automotive Complex site
Used cars (open space)

Industrial area (offices)
Park (landscape)
Residential area

9

0   500m

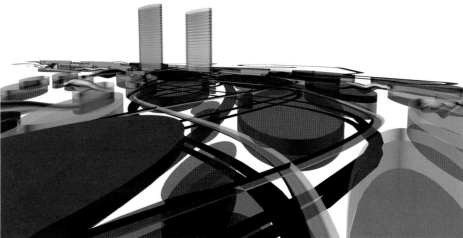

10

6 *Despite its apparently free forms, the complex has a carefully considered design*   7 *The curved design is evident in the model view*   8 *Seen from another angle, the model shows the relief of the forms against the flat, desert background*   9 *An overall plan of the complex with the different elements clearly delineated*   10 *Roads connect different elements of the complex as seen in this layered rendering*

Automotive Showroom and Leisure Center

Cairo, Egypt, 2008–2011

Manuelle Gautrand

This 12,000-square-metre complex for Ghabbour Auto, to be located in the new Allegria district of the Egyptian capital, includes showrooms for several different automobile brands as well as leisure facilities such as cafés, a food court and two movie theatres. Having based her idea on the rotating turntable presentations often seen at car fairs, Manuelle Gautrand explains that the volume was 'conceived with the circle as a starting point, and develops itself in a vast sculpture of circles and spheres, which are stuck together. The intersection between them creates all the circulation patterns, atriums, and visual perspectives throughout the building'.

Flexibility, allowing for showrooms and other facilities to be moved as required, was another key element in this design. The basic showroom module is 80 square metres, with the possibility of combining several modules to create a larger space. A long atrium runs through the centre of the building. The architect imagined a 'pale and delicate' or 'pearly white' concrete structure with bright colours in the VIP lounge, media lounge, cafés and sales spaces. Two horizontal lines of LEDs representing the brand names encircle the floors, giving coloured movement behind the glass façade.

1 *The longitudinal section is characterised by large-scale round openings* **Opposite** *The interior design uses cutouts and sweeping forms to provide unexpected views of the vehicles on display*

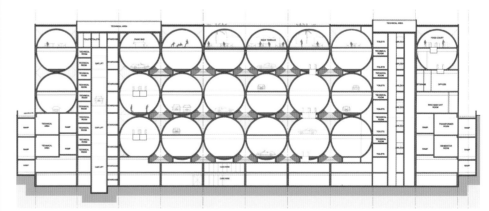

1

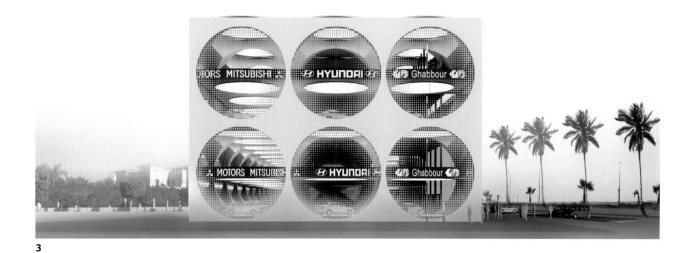

3

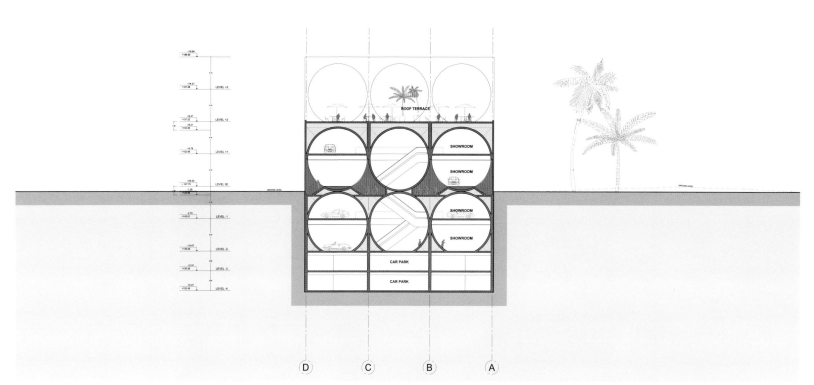

4

5

3 *Side elevation rendering showing the use of car brands in the circular cutouts in the façade*   4 *Section drawing of the building from the same angle with showroom spaces below grade as well as a two-storey car park*   5 *Rendering of the main façade with car brands and entrance area (left)*   6 *Night rendering of the showroom from a side angle; the main, rectangular entrance is in the centre*

6

7 *Round openings alternate with hexagonal ones, while sweeping escalators carry customers between levels* **8** *The tent-like seating area features Eastern-inspired geometric designs* **9** *Rendering showing the seating area from ground level*

7

9

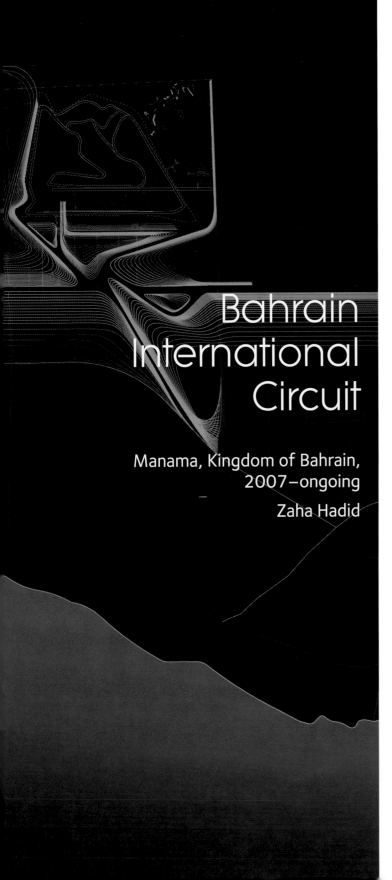

Bahrain International Circuit

Manama, Kingdom of Bahrain,
2007–ongoing
–
Zaha Hadid

This very large project, covering an area of more than 1000 hectares on a site with an existing Formula One racetrack, includes a hotel, conference centre, car showrooms, a master plan for a research centre, a high-end car manufacturing plant and a university. The site is characterised by a rough yellow desert rock. Given the size of the project, it is clear that Hadid's ongoing interest in the topographical element of architecture is being firmly engaged here. Furthermore, the design is carefully thought out to engage and intertwine the driving experience and the architecture.

According to Hadid, 'As one approaches the car experience development with its hotels, showcases, and the car and activity-oriented programs, additional roads bring one into close interaction with the architecture. Flitting above the architecture and diving below it, ramping past the iconic new buildings and coming into and out of view, the cars on the site dance through the landscape, interact with the buildings, and add to the visual drama of movement on the site'.

The architect has imagined the buildings as a series of oases or 'jewels' set into the landscape. Her high-tech and streamlined design emerges from the meeting of the site and its function. Hadid explains that the Bahrain International Circuit proposes 'a new choreography of automobiles, architecture and landscape'.

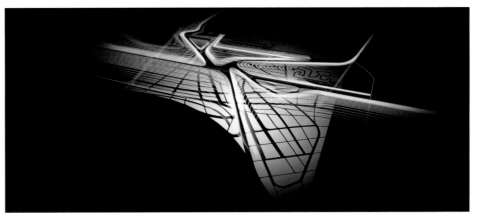

1

2

3

1 *Hadid's drawing speaks more of lines of force than an explicit rendering of the architectural forms*   2 *An overall view of the complex showing how the forms and the circuit flow into one another seamlessly*   3 *Drawing demonstrating the fluid interaction between the architecture and the domain of the automobiles*   4 *Drawing showing the long, low-lying buildings with the viewing stands on the left*

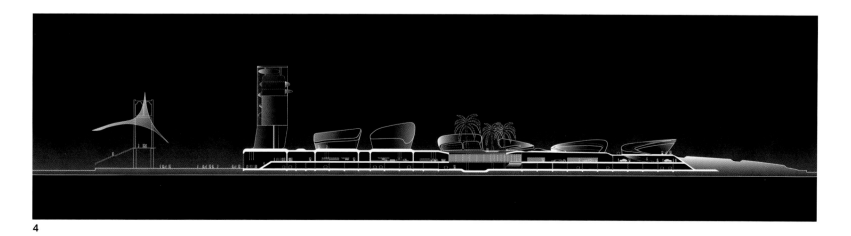

4

5

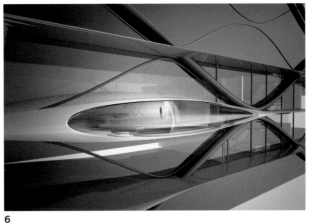

6

7

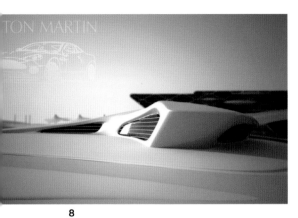

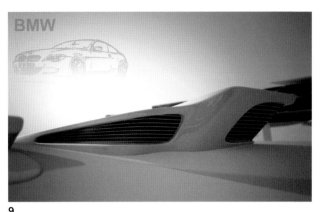

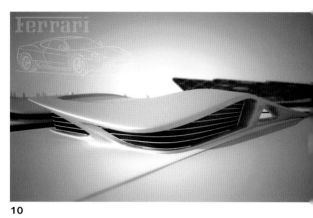

8   9   10

5 *Buildings in the complex look almost like speeding vehicles*   **6** *A façade view showing the dynamic, stretched forms employed to unify the architecture and to convey an image of speed*   **7** *An interior rendering explains how interior and exterior spaces are a coherent part of a whole*   **8, 9, 10** *Spaces are assigned to particular car manufacturers*   **11** *The succession of forms imagined by Hadid occupy spaces like a natural geological or biological formation*

11

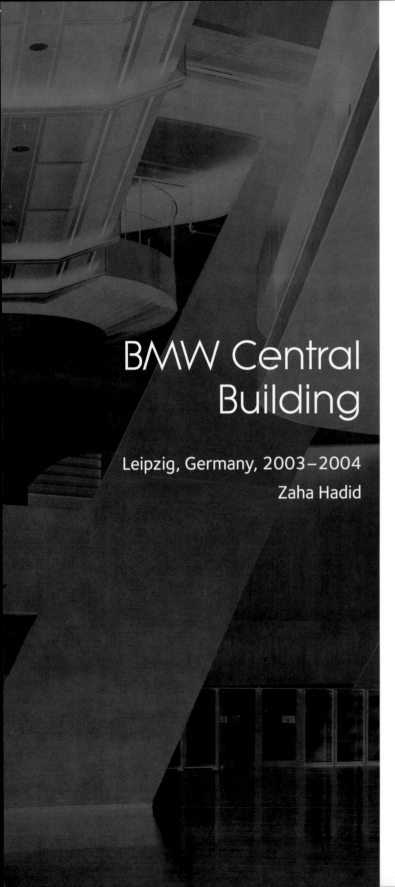

BMW Central Building

Leipzig, Germany, 2003–2004

Zaha Hadid

Zaha Hadid was asked to design the BMW Central Building, the 'nerve centre' of the entire factory complex as well as its entrance, after winning a 2002 competition. A large number of prefabricated elements, provided by suppliers also called on for the BMW factory, were used in the design, in part because the car manufacturer required an industrial approach to the office spaces.

The facility connects the three principal manufacturing departments of the factory. Hadid's intention was to create a transparent internal organisation, while allowing the different functions to meet in order to avoid segregating status groups.

The cascading floor system in this structure, made with self-compacting concrete and a roof assembled with a series of steel H-beams, allows users and visitors to view the different parts of the manufacturing process, giving a clear indication that each element contributes to an integrated process.

According to the architect, 'It was the client's objective to translate industrial architecture into an aesthetic concept that complies equally with representational and functional requirements. In the transition zones between manufacturing halls and public space, the Central Building acts as a mediator, impressing a positive permanent impact upon the eye of the beholder in a restrained, semiotic way'.

Opposite *This impressive view of the building's underside translates its mass while providing a dynamic impression*

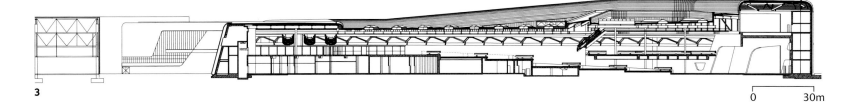

3

0   30m

Opposite *The architect has carefully crafted the volumes to allow the building to fit into the plant*   **3** *Elevation showing the long, low volume that rises gradually on one side*

4 *The structure steps high over a parking area, like a great moving vehicle*

4

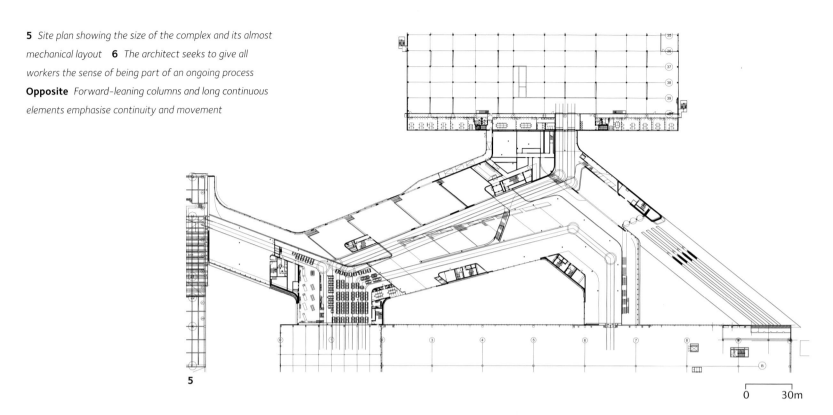

5

0   30m

6

8

9

8 *Views penetrate through the various spaces*   **9** *Looking up through the complex interior spaces that connect the different parts of the building*

Opposite *Some parts of the architecture resemble elevated roads that may indeed carry cars in the process of being manufactured*

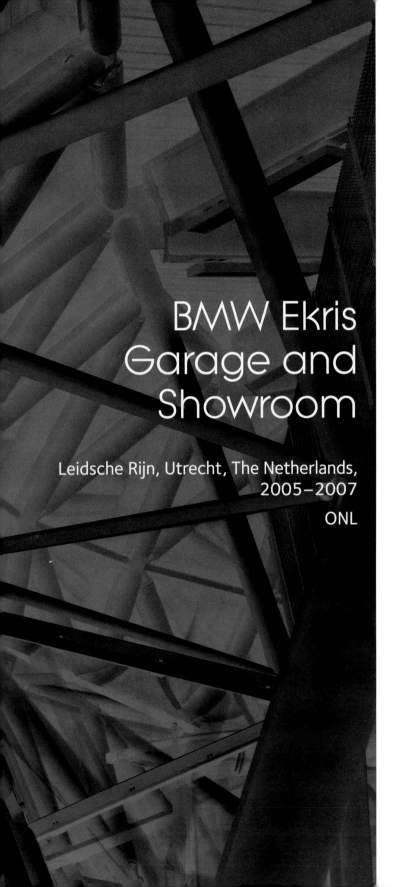

BMW Ekris Garage and Showroom

Leidsche Rijn, Utrecht, The Netherlands,
2005–2007
ONL

Behind the Acoustic Barrier and the Hessing Cockpit (page 106), ONL created two mirror-image buildings for BMW. The design for the two 11,800-square-metre structures is directly related to the forms of the automobile. Their shape refers to the BMW's two signature kidney-shaped grilles with slightly tilted bars.

With its structural monocoque concept, the BMW Ekris Garage and Showroom has another direct relationship to automobile design. As the architects explained, 'The design for the BMW Ekris Showroom is in all styling aspects a 3D volume like the modern car body itself'. The swept-back or forward-leaning appearance of the structure also implies movement, another obvious feature of vehicular transport. More specifically, the architects used the headlights of the BMW 5 Series as a reference for the large glazed section that rounds off the street-facing corner of the building.

1 *Sketch showing the overall form of the building* **2** *The completed structure with its tall glazing closely resembles the original sketch*

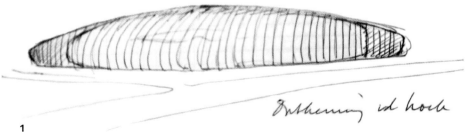

1

2

3 *The bulbous, outward-leaning skin rises up at ground level to reveal the cars within*   **4** *Section showing that the structure's basic forms are relatively straightforward inside*

5 *The diamond-shaped glazing that covers the entire structure on one side makes it glow from within after nightfall*   **6** *A more distant night view of the garage and showroom*

3

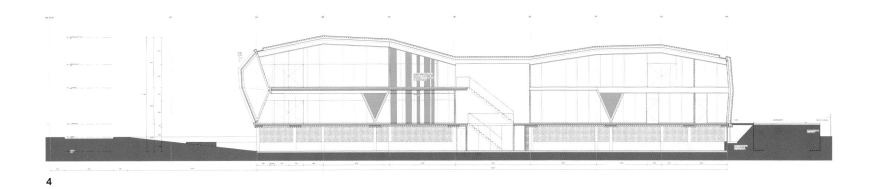

4

5

6

7

8

9

7 *Interior spaces leave ample column-free space for the display and parking of cars* **8** *Vehicles are shown here on two levels, with the space frame supporting the main window volumes seen to the right* **9** *Articulated supports for the windows are echoed by the V-shaped support of the mezzanine level* **10** *A view through the complex web that supports the walls and ceiling of the structure* **11** *Detail of node that unites support elements* **12** *A basic plan shows the rounded-square form of the building*

10

11

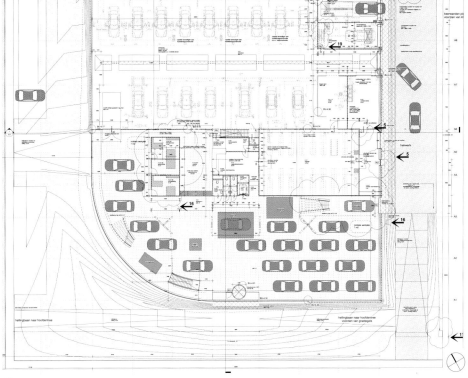

12

BMW Museum

Munich, Germany, 2003
ATELIER BRÜCKNER

The BMW Museum in Munich opened in 2008. Along with the BMW Welt (see page 68), which opened in October 2007, and the BMW factory tour, the museum is the final component of the BMW Triad, which is expected to receive two million visitors annually. Stuttgart studio ATELIER BRÜCKNER was commissioned for the general planning, architecture and exhibition design. ART+COM, a Berlin design office for new media, conceived the spatial media design and interactive installations, while Integral Ruedi Baur developed the graphic design.

A ramp system is the central element for the architecture and exhibition spaces. On this ramp, which according to ATELIER BRÜCKNER was made to resemble a street-like path of polished asphalt, the visitor is steered into the BMW Museum. Surrounded by refined automobile-inspired architectural scenery, an uninterrupted kilometre-long walkway leads the visitor through the permanent exhibition and Museum Bowl spaces. The ramp system resembles a three-dimensional road that provides access to the exhibition houses on different floors.

The climax of the tour is the BMW Platz, developed by ATELIER BRÜCKNER with ART+COM. Visible several times during the tour of the museum, this 13-metre-high space features glass façades imbedded with 1.7 million LEDs, creating a total of 30 possible light displays. As is the case with ATELIER BRÜCKNER's Shanghai Auto Museum, the BMW Museum employs the city and the road as metaphors that organise the automobile experience and displays. With an exhibition space of 5000 square metres and a total area of 10,000 square metres, the museum shows 125 cars, motorcycles, aircraft and racing engines in 25 different areas.

Opposite *The display space inside the museum imparts a very modern feeling, even to cars that are considerably older than the architecture*

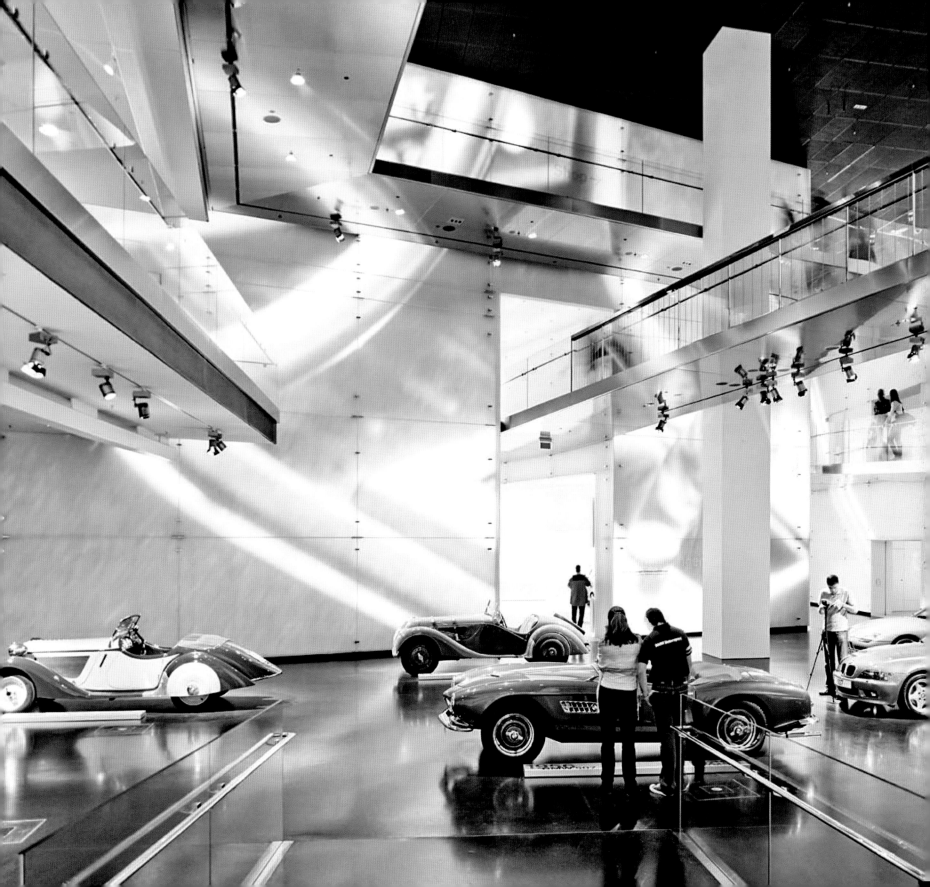

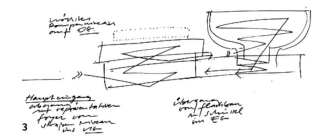

3

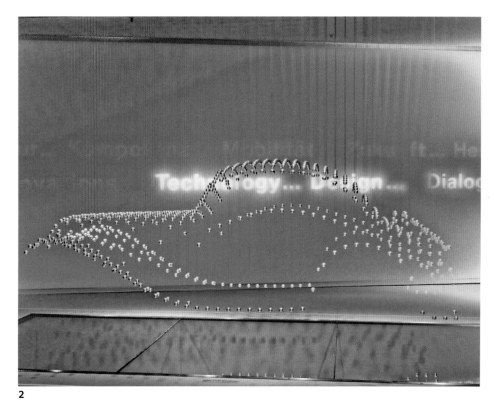

2

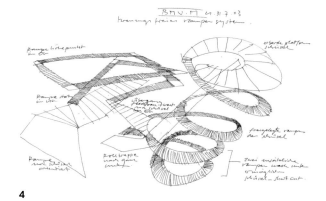

4

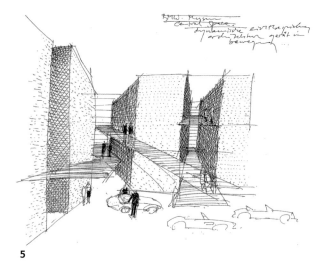

5

2 *Exhibition design focuses on the interaction of technical and aesthetic elements*   **3** *Sketch showing a section view of the building and its internal circulation*   **4** *Visitor circulation through the space*   **5** *Scale and the contrast between opacity and transparency are suggested in this sketch*   **6** *A model of the building shows a full section with display areas, ramps and escalators visible*

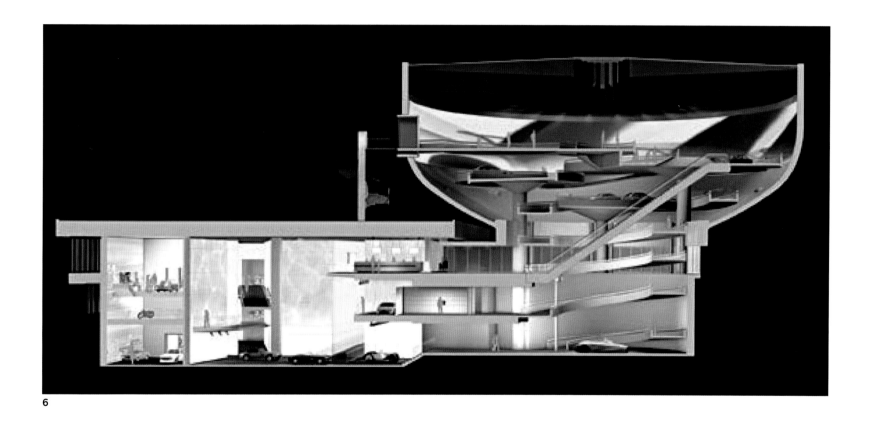

6

1975
BMW 3.0 CSL

Systematic participation in touring-car events began when BMW Motorsport was established. The BMW 3.0 CSL factory-entered cars with their characteristic striped look and large front and rear spoilers soon became a familiar sight on the international touring-car racing scene, and took the European championship title in 1973. After a year in which restraint was exercised due to the oil crisis, activities in 1975 were concentrated on factory entries for the American IMSA race series. The European championship title went to these cars in five further seasons between 1975 and 1979. At first with a 3.0- or 3.3-litre engine, later with a 3.5-litre unit with four valves per cylinder, the BMW 3.0 CSL was among the most powerful cars on the starting grid. Systematic development work and turbo-charging boosted engine output to as much as 750 bhp.

8

Opposite *Race cars and motorcycles are displayed one above the other, emphasising the firm's tradition in this area* **8** *Photos and trophies are displayed alongside the corresponding BMW race vehicles*

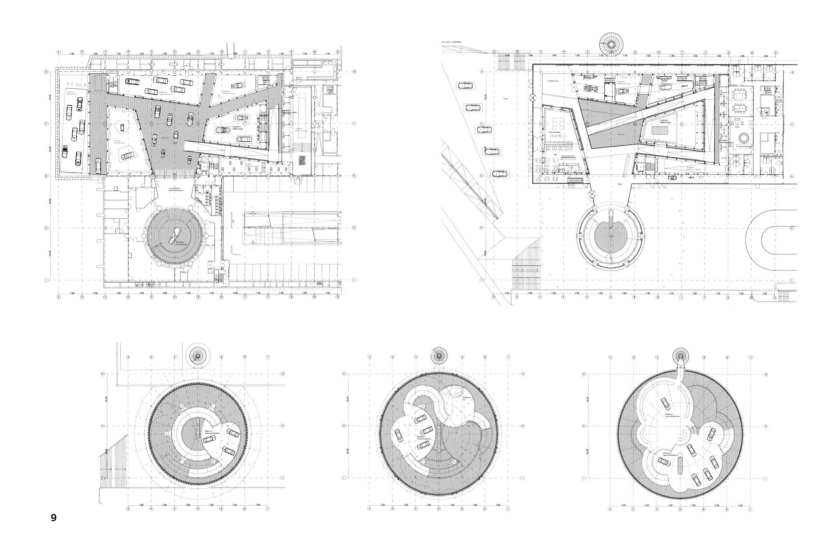

9 Floor plans and drawings showing circulation and the arrangement of vehicles in the circular area on the plans   **10** Generous ceiling heights and views through the spaces contribute to an overall concept and design coherence   **11** Older cars are aligned in an immaculate space that suggests how precious these vehicles have become   **12** Ramps and bridges connect the spaces while offering glimpses of other areas below and beyond   **13** Motors are displayed like works of art and explained to the layman   **14** An individual vehicle is spotlighted and set apart like any masterpiece might be in a museum of art   **15** A café and bar space in the museum; design continuity stretches from the display spaces into this area

10

11

12

13

14

15

BMW Welt

Munich, Germany, 2001–2007
COOP HIMMELB(L)AU

One of a series of large new automobile delivery centres with exhibition space for German automobile manufacturers, BMW Welt is a 70,000-square-metre facility that cost more than €100 million to build. It has a total of seven floors, with the area underground exceeding the area above grade. Austrian architects COOP HIMMELB(L)AU won the 2001 competition with their design for this project, which began construction in 2003 and opened in 2007.

The lead architect, Wolf D. Prix, describes the project: 'The concept behind the design envisions a hybrid building representing a mixture of urban elements. Not an exhibition hall, not an information and communication centre, not a museum, but instead all of these things, along a passage organised under one roof and horizontally and vertically layered. A conjoining of urban marketplace and stage for presentations'.

The powerful and dynamic design greets approximately 850,000 visitors each year and is paired with the BMW Museum by ATELIER BRÜCKNER (see page 60). Supported only by its elevator shafts and 11 columns, the building is something of an engineering feat as well as a spectacular space for the exhibition of cars, and for events such as culinary gatherings in the Cone element of the structure.

1 *In this night view, the building appears to resemble a moving vortex of energy, glowing from within*

1

2 *Looking like something out of a science fiction film, the building arches high over the exterior space*   **3** *Section showing the complexity of the building's different levels, and the vortex-like shape at the entrance (left)*   **4** *The impression of movement is accentuated by both structural elements and the cladding*

2

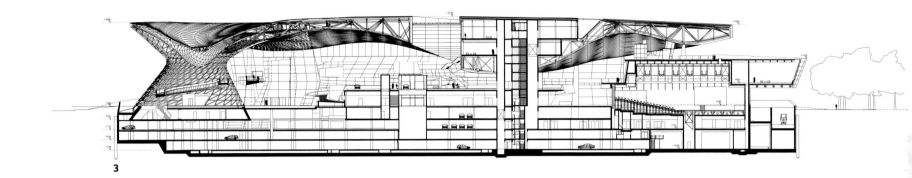

3

4

5 *From certain angles, the building looks like nothing else ever built, and yet it conserves a practical, functional side* **6** *An orchestration of angled surfaces and elements provides a continuing impression of movement through space* **7** *A section through the building gives an idea of its impressive scale and the variation of spaces within* **8** *The idea of a vortex is also present within the building* **9** *A web of supports appears to swirl around a central roof element, being drawn in as if by the force of gravity* **10** *A view of the roof cladding and its wave form*

5

6

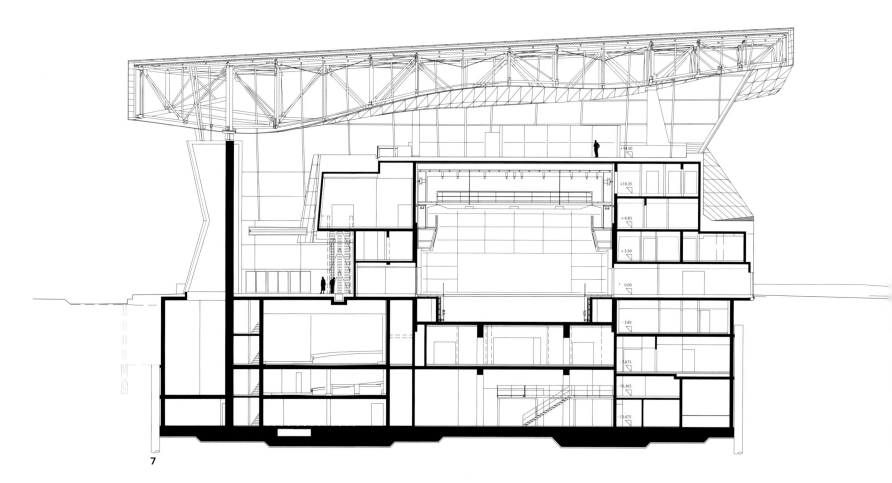

7

8

9

10

11 *Interior spaces are as generous as the large exterior volume suggests* **12** *Site plan* **13** *The architecture emphasises views through the complex and generously proportioned interior volumes* **14** *Further evidence of the vortex effect of the architecture*

11

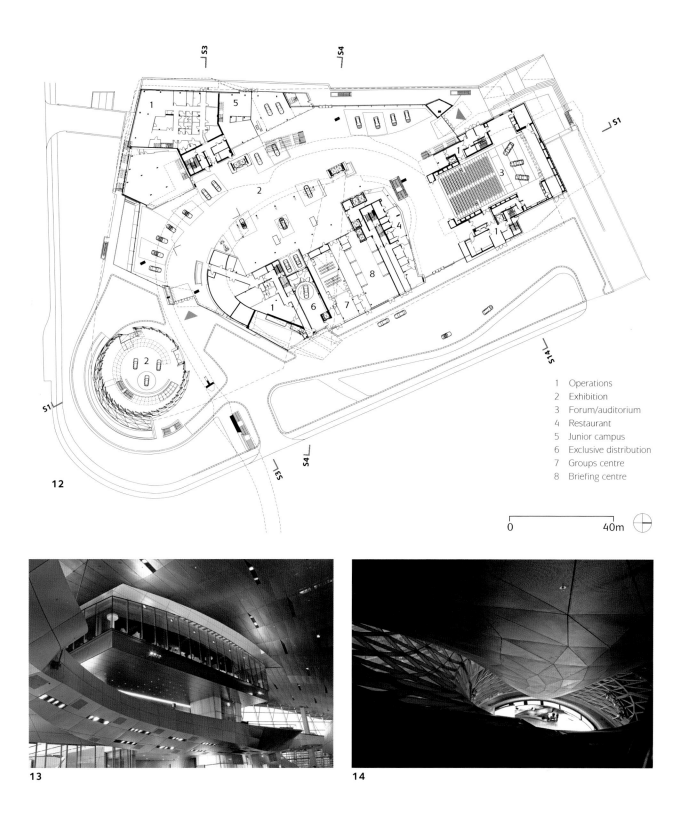

1   Operations
2   Exhibition
3   Forum/auditorium
4   Restaurant
5   Junior campus
6   Exclusive distribution
7   Groups centre
8   Briefing centre

0   40m

12

13   **14**

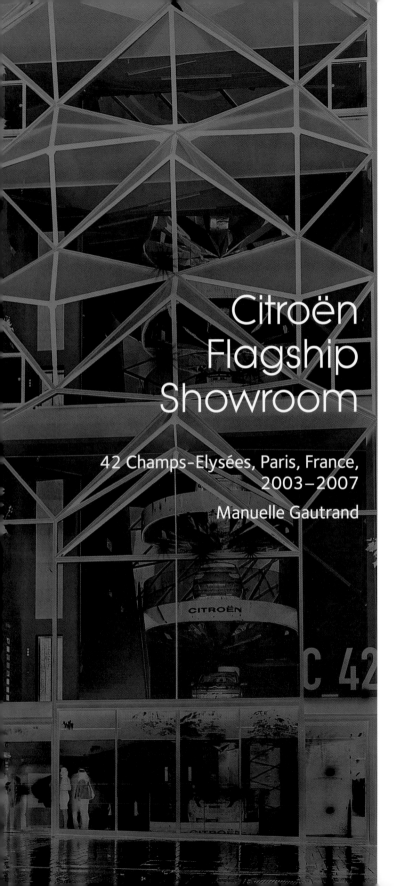

Citroën Flagship Showroom

42 Champs-Elysées, Paris, France, 2003–2007

Manuelle Gautrand

French architect Manuelle Gautrand won the 2002 competition for this project, which included entries from the likes of Zaha Hadid, Daniel Libeskind and Christian de Portzamparc, to rebuild one of the most prestigious automobile-related sites in Paris for Citroën Automobiles.

Citroën first installed a showroom at 42 Champs-Elysées in 1927. In 1931, the firm called on its factory designer Ravazé and its art director Pierre Louÿs to redesign the building.

Gautrand was commissioned to entirely rebuild the 1200-square-metre structure. She designed a complex glass façade for the Champs-Elysées side of the building using a somewhat abstracted version of Citroën's inverted double-V symbol as a leitmotif. This glass façade reveals a series of suspended platforms where the firm's cars are exhibited. These platforms allow for a generous space despite the long, narrow site that the architect had to work with. Gautrand was inspired by the words of the car designer Pininfarina: 'Citroën means non-aggressive performance'.

Opposite *The stacked display platforms of the Citroën showroom on the Champs-Elysées in Paris*

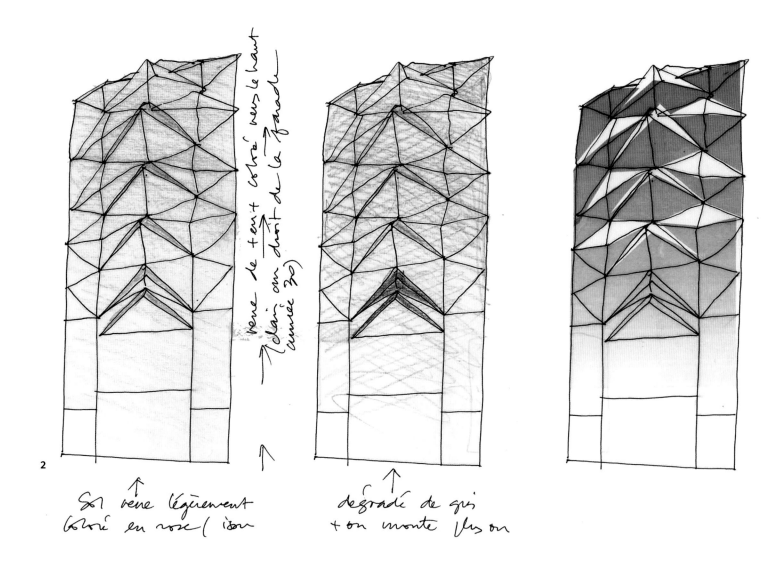

2

3

4

6

7

8

Opposite *The rotating platforms open onto relatively modest-sized display spaces on each level* **6** *Service desk and displays* **7** *A display platform facing the main glazed façade on the Champs-Elysées* **8** *Round display platforms allow the cars to be seen from every angle as visitors move up or down through the building*

9 *Looking out to the Champs-Elysées entrance* **10** *A section drawing shows the suspended display platforms and the viewing spaces for visitors* **11** *The light colour patterns of the building contrast with the darker main support of the display platforms* **12** *Extensive glazing floods the display area and stairway with natural light* **13** *A vintage car contrasts with the modern lines of the building* **14** *The double chevron logo pattern is also visible from the interior of the showroom*

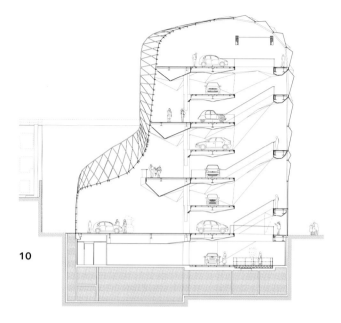

10

9

11

82

12

13

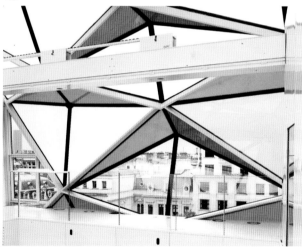

14

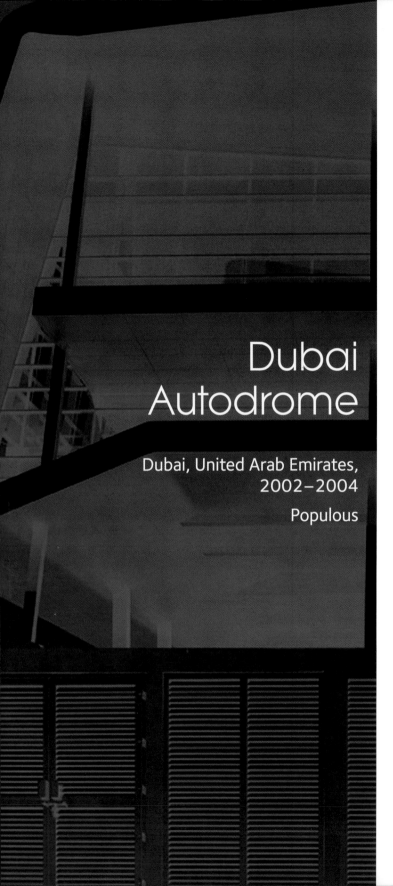

Dubai Autodrome

Dubai, United Arab Emirates,
2002–2004

Populous

The Dubai Autodrome is located on a 279-hectare desert site about half an hour outside Dubai. The circuit's marketing and management building with a viewing gallery, office and conference room was the first structure completed – the 7000-seat grandstand and racetrack following shortly thereafter. The 5.39-kilometre track can be used in six different configurations and the complex includes a race and driving school as well as a carting track.

The nature of the facility is such that it can be used for other events such as large concerts. According to the architect, the architectural style of this complex and its signature marketing and management building draw from concepts central to motor sports and racing. Chief among these is the idea of dynamic balance – that fine line between speed and traction, between motion and control. Dynamic balance is achieved on the track when a driver balances the centrifugal force of corners and pushes the limits of possibility. The marketing and management building captures that feeling with a structure that appears active, figuratively 'leaning into the turns'. The dynamic balance established in the marketing and management building's design is echoed in other buildings throughout the complex. This creates a continuity of form from building to building, and makes the development instantly recognisable.

Opposite *The raked form of the viewing gallery*

2

3

4

5

2 & 3 *The marketing and management building seen from two different angles*   4 *The main grandstands have generous canopies to protect viewers from the harsh desert sun*   5 *The forward-leaning aspect of the architecture is well suited to its speed-oriented purpose*

6

7

8

6 *The architecture is based on a single folded sheet form, bent and cantilevered according to its function* **7** *The sweeping forms of the buildings are attuned to the racecourse function and imply movement* **8** *The modernity and strength of the buildings stand out from the desert environment* **9** *Graphics emphasise the rapid movement of the cars* **10** *The main grandstand in the background with the circuit in the foreground*

9

10

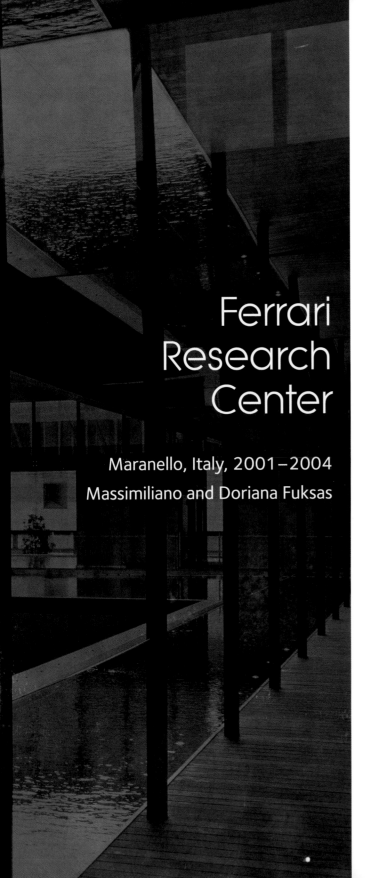

Ferrari Research Center

Maranello, Italy, 2001–2004

Massimiliano and Doriana Fuksas

Built in the centre of the Ferrari complex in Maranello, the 17,000-square-metre Ferrari Research Center sits between the firm's wind tunnel and the mechanics' building. The architect, working with his wife and partner Doriana Mandrelli Fuksas for the interiors and artistic direction, has sought what he calls 'new poetics of lightness', using light, water and bamboo to integrate the architecture into its natural environment. An overhanging volume is suspended above a pond that covers the lower elements of the design. This volume extends 7 metres over the entrance area.

Fuksas writes, 'Above the surface of the water various walkways create a network of connections between two meeting rooms, marked by their respective colours, that is, red and yellow. Water and light are the kinetic elements of the building, designating space with reflections that give the upper volume the impression of a precious metal container. In the middle of the building, a precisely ordered rectangular bamboo forest filters light and reflects it in a thousand different directions'.

1 *Architect's sketch*   **Opposite** *External view at night*

1

3

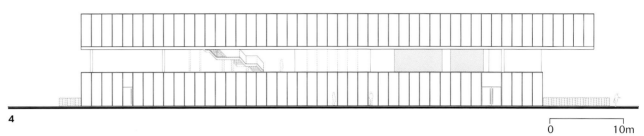

4

0   10m

3 *View of the court with footbridge over the water*   **4** *Elevation*   **5** *General view of the complex*
6 *Detail of inner façade*

5

6

7 *The steel structure*   **8 & Opposite** *Views of the court and pool of water*

10

12   **13**

10 *Detail of internal office spaces*   **11** *View of the court*   **12** *Detail of the glass wall opening onto the 'red' meeting room*   **13** *The system of ramps and vertical ascents in the inner courtyards*
14 *Ground floor plan*

11

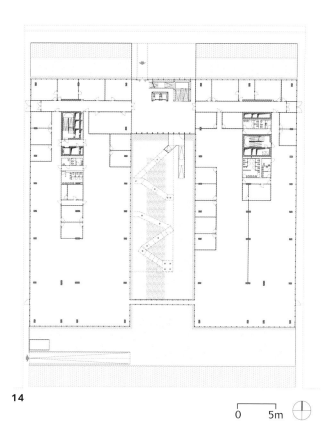

14

0   5m

Helios House

Los Angeles, California, USA,
2006–2007

Office dA, Johnston Marklee
and BIG at Ogilvy & Mather

It might seem difficult to imagine a 'green' service station, but firms such as BP, the client for Helios House, have in fact invested substantial sums in research and development of cleaner fuels. With a floor area of 975 square metres, Helios House is intended to encourage dialogue and education on the subject of environmental stewardship.

Set at the corner of Robertson and Olympic Boulevards, the station (Architect of Record: Johnston Marklee) has a triangulated prefabricated steel panel structure. Recycled materials, energy-efficient lights and 90 solar panels are some of the energy strategies adopted, reducing the building's consumption of energy by 16 percent, compared to a more traditional structure of the same size. While referring to the tradition of service station architecture in the US, the architects have succeeded in renewing the genre and asking the right questions about the responsibility of large corporations such as BP.

Opposite *The faceted shell of the structure immediately signals that it is unlike other service stations*

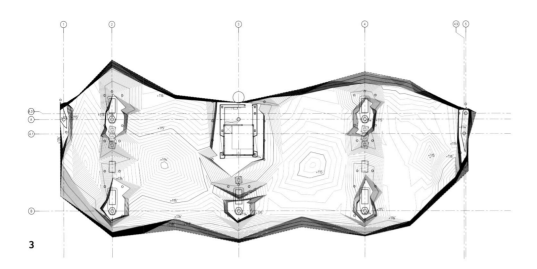

3

Opposite *Helios House assumes an almost organic form from this angle, as the 'petal to the metal' sign suggests*   **3** *The site plan reads almost like a topographic map, emphasising the organic concept*   **4** *An overhanging sign projects above the faceted, tree-like structure*

4

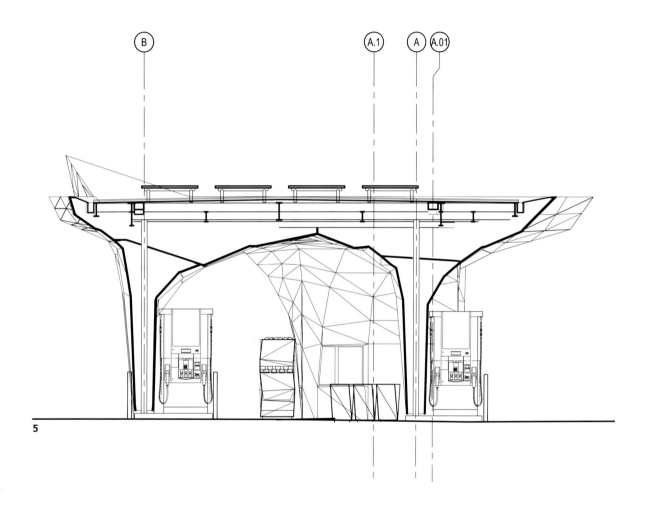

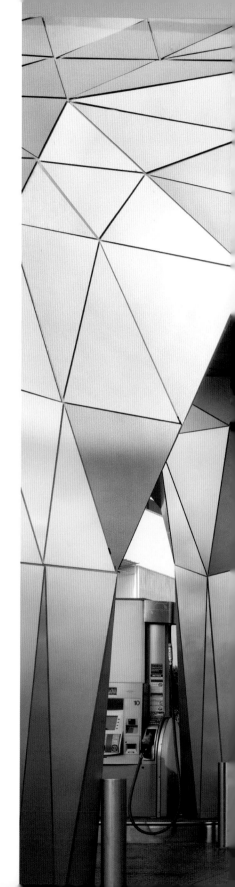

5 *Despite its faceted design, the basic structure functions like an elaborate shed* **Opposite** *The structural pattern of Helios House is applied to both its exterior faces and the underside*

8

9

Opposite *The structure is unique in its urban Los Angeles setting*
8 *The facets of the design envelope form interior elements just
as they define the main canopy* **9** *The cladding patterns, which
correspond to the structure itself, seem to have a life of their own*

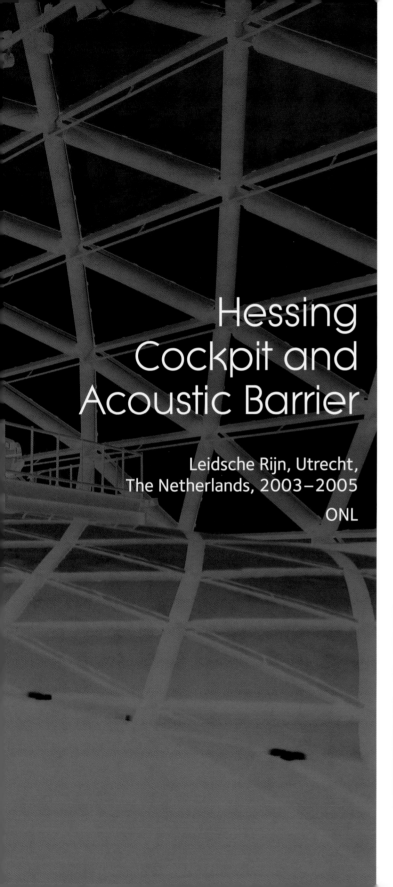

Hessing Cockpit and Acoustic Barrier

Leidsche Rijn, Utrecht,
The Netherlands, 2003–2005

ONL

Although in some sense distinct, the Hessing Cockpit and Acoustic Barrier designed by ONL are part of the same structure. Set along the heavily travelled A2 Highway near Utrecht, the Acoustic Barrier is a 1.5-kilometre-long structure with a surface area of 10,800 square metres. Ten times longer than it is high, the overall Acoustic Barrier is designed with the 120-kilometre-per-hour speed of passing vehicles in mind. It was important both to fulfil the functional requirement of blocking out the sound of the highway and to avoid motorists slowing down or causing accidents because they are distracted.

Parametric modelling and computer-driven manufacturing methods were used to design and build the complex curves of the building, allowing for the creation of unique pieces ready to be bolted together. Set within the Acoustic Barrier, the Hessing Cockpit is a 6400-square-metre automobile showroom and sales point for four luxury car brands: Rolls Royce and Bentley, Lamborghini, Maserati and Lotus. The building has four levels connected by a 'closed-circuit loop' allowing vehicular access to each floor.

1 This façade view emphasises the long, low form of the building, as seen from the highway   2 Elevations show the building's relatively simple concept   3 The Hessing Cockpit and Acoustic Barrier seen at night from the highway side

1

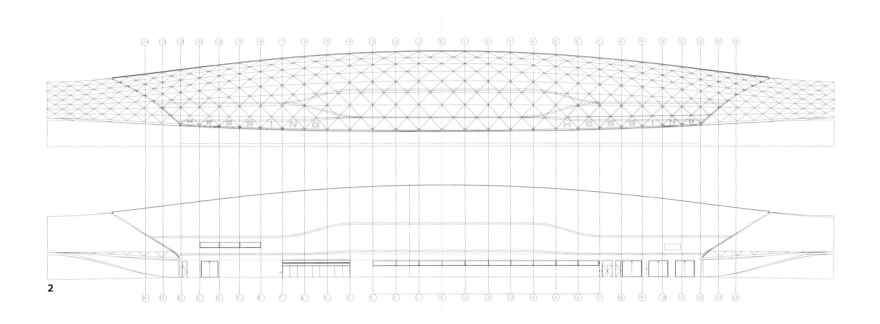

2

3

4 *The dense structural web is the result of a computer-generated design, which also guided the manufacture of the parts* 5 *The radiating forms of the glazing and supports reflect a design that would have been very difficult to build before computer-assisted methods were developed* 6 *Section showing the support elements of the structure*

4

5

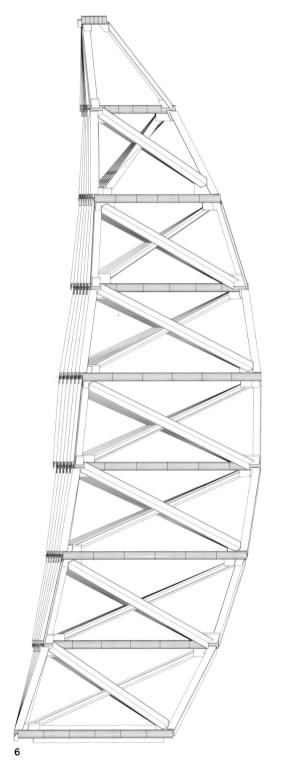

6

7 The interior of the structure with its broad areas for the display of vehicles and the main curving, glazed façade   **8** A section shows the main glazed façade to the right, with the more orthogonal interior floors   **9** The curve of the building emphasises the impression of speed   **10** The lines of this car seem perfectly suited to the large sweeping curves of the architecture   **11** Speed is expressed in the form of the building just as it is in the cars displayed or those passing outside   **12** Bright, generous space characterises the inside of the building

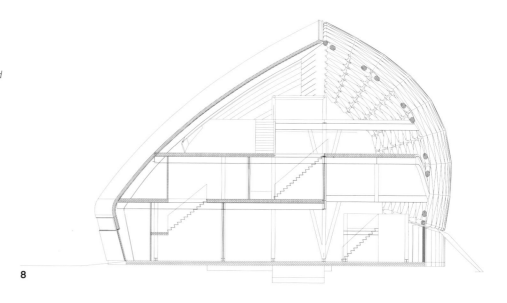

8

7

9

10

11

12

In-N-Out Burger Westwood

Los Angeles, California, USA, 1998
Kanner Architects

Located in the northwest corner of the Westwood Village district of Los Angeles, near the UCLA campus, this prototype fast-food restaurant offered a vivid new image for the 50-year-old iconic burger chain. The building was completed in March 1998. Founded in 1948, the popular In-N-Out Burger chain was housed in mostly modest roadside structures. They were the first to offer ordering via a two-way speaker and introduced the idea of drive-through windows where customers could pull up in their cars and watch their order being prepared.

The 418-square-metre structure's design integrates the boomerang shape and colours of the company's logo. As Stephen Kanner explains, 'Making a sign into a building and blowing it up in scale is very much a part of roadside architecture'. In this sense, despite its very contemporary feeling, the building relates to the 1950s tradition of American road buildings, when roadside architecture was designed to grab the attention of motorists. Here, the folded form lifts up to allow for ample glazing that permits visitors to see the cooking going on inside. This restaurant quickly became the chain's third-best performing location out of more than 150, proving that a strong architectural statement can be good for business.

1 *The form of the structure and the arrow above draw customers in, as does the colour scheme*

1

2

2 *The architecture accommodates existing trees*   3 *The angled, very contemporary forms of the In-N-Out burger structure seem to go far beyond the design consciousness of other similar facilities*

3

1 Main entrance
2 Dining area
3 Outdoor patio
4 Cashier
5 Kitchen
6 Drive-up order menu
7 Drive-through
8 Order window
9 Pick-up window
10 Restroom
11 Lift
12 Staff parking
13 Garbage
14 Storage
15 Ramp

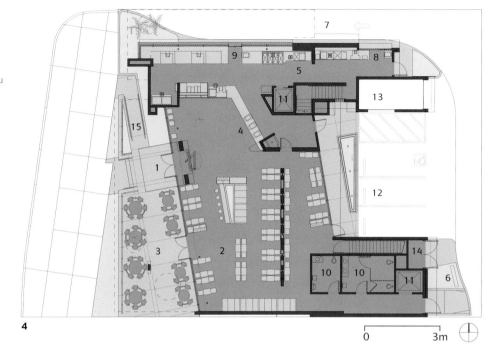

4

0   3m

5

4 *Floor plan showing the vehicle arrival area at the top* 5 *Seen at nightfall, the V-shaped arrow sign becomes a theme of the building, implying the rapidity of service* 6 *The strong colours and graphics of the exterior influence the interior*

6

I-WAY

Lyon, France, 2008
Agence Cyrille Druart

Inaugurated in July 2008 in Lyon, France, I-WAY is a building devoted to automobile simulations inspired by the aeronautics industry. The structure is laid out on three levels and there are three simulation zones (Formula 1, Endurance, Rally/Touring) as well as a fitness room, an alcohol-free bar that features a 10-metre counter made of Corian, like most of the furniture, a bar/restaurant lounge with terraces, two conference rooms, meeting rooms and offices. A total of 18 vehicles are also on display. The main activities are located on the first floor, including the simulation zones that are conceived as empty concrete cubes. The designer Cyrille Druart (born in 1980 in Paris) describes the structure as an 'impenetrable box' that willfully hides its functions. He states, 'It is a box that collapses and huddles in a heap during the day and comes to life at night thanks to its lighting, through a rigid plastic skin. Based on a centripetal design, the building focuses inward on itself.'

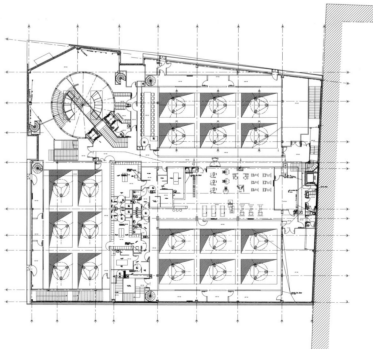

1

1 *First floor plan* **2** *The exterior of the I-WAY building contrasts black and white blocks*

2

3

4

5

6

3 *Simulators set up in racecar replicas* **4** *A walkway provides access to the simulator spaces* **5** *Formula One race simulators aligned in I-WAY* **6** *The Lounge Bar with a 4-metre truncated cone in black Corian and restaurant offering gourmet food* **7** *The massage room with heated Corian tables designed exclusively for I-WAY* **8** *The White Bar with a 10-metre long white Corian bar*

7

8

Lingotto Factory Conversion

Turin, Italy, 1983–2003
Renzo Piano Building Workshop

Renzo Piano worked for 30 years on the rehabilitation of Fiat's Lingotto Factory in Turin. Built between 1917 and 1920 by the engineer Giacomo Mattè Trucco, the Lingotto Factory was praised by Le Corbusier in his 1923 manifesto *Vers une architecture*. Piano decided at the outset to maintain the basic characteristics of the building. Between 1992 and 1995, he added a heliport and bubble panoramic meeting room to the former factory. Between 1990 and 1994, a concert hall was added. More recently, in 2002, Piano added the Giovanni and Marella Agnelli Art Gallery to the former automobile plant.

Giovanni Agnelli explained, 'Those who come to visit Lingotto will see an area on the outskirts of Turin – between the Alps and the hill on which the city stands – that I have always loved. One of Renzo Piano's special gifts as an architect is that his designs seem to inject new life into the area around a new building, a new project; the entire place becomes a sort of resonance chamber for the building under construction. The houses, the urban fabric, the metropolis itself become a sort of network, at the centre of which the traveller finds a moment of aesthetic repose and reflection'.

1 *Aerial view of the revitalised complex*   **2** *The factory prior to rehabilitation*   **3** *Façade detail: the architect sought to maintain the monumental character of the building*

1

2

3

123

4

5

6

4 *The glass-domed conference 'bubble' and helipad are visible from a distance, updating the futuristic aspect of the original building* **5** *View of the Lingotto Factory after the rehabilitation* **6** *Interior of the glass-domed conference room* **7** *Ramp leading to the track on the roof, a characteristic feature of the Lingotto complex* **8** *Passage through the garden known as 'Giardino delle Meraviglie'* **9** *Interior of the auditorium, conceived as a musical instrument lined with solid cherry wood* **10** *Concert and congress hall in use for public rehearsal of a symphony orchestra concert as seen from choir seats behind stage*

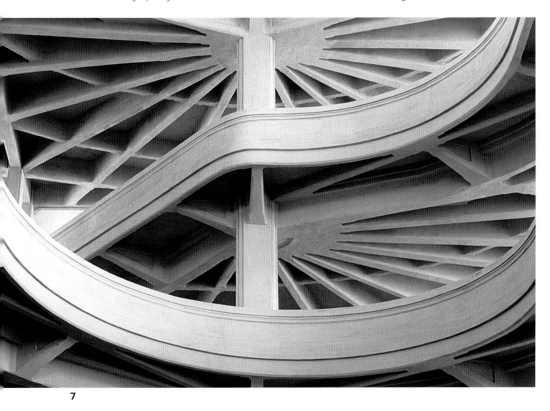

7

8

9

10

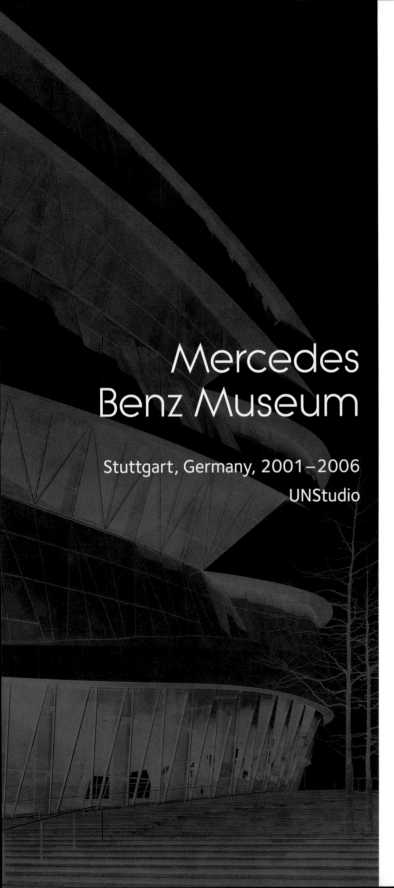

Mercedes Benz Museum

Stuttgart, Germany, 2001–2006

UNStudio

This exceptional 53,000-square-metre museum is set on the grounds of Mercedes Benz's historic Untertürkheim manufacturing plant, near the B14 highway entering Stuttgart. Amsterdam firm UNStudio won the 2002 international architectural competition to design the nine-level concrete structure, which features a 47-metre-high atrium and double-helix-inspired interior ramps. These ramps and the layout of the display spaces allow for different yet intersecting stories of the brand's development.

Ben van Berkel of UNStudio worked with well-known Stuttgart engineer Werner Sobek on the project and also called on talented exhibition designer H.G. Merz, Amsterdam designer Petra Blaisse (Inside-Outside) and Concrete Architectural Associates for interior design elements.

Sophisticated parametric modelling was used together with entirely new software that contributed to the generation of 38,000 working drawings. The experience of moving through the museum is dynamic, heightened by occasional views towards the busy highway that lies just past the building. Mobility is thus inscribed in both the actual situation of the building and its interior circulation patterns.

Opposite *The exterior of the museum with its irregular bands is visible from a busy highway and from the Mercedes assembly plant*

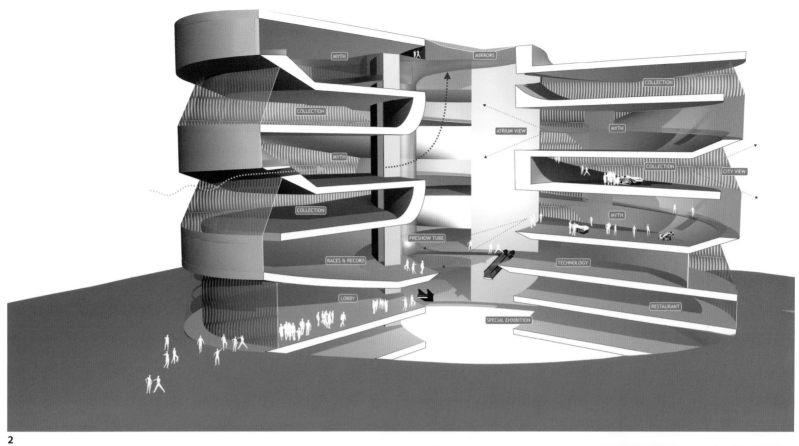

2

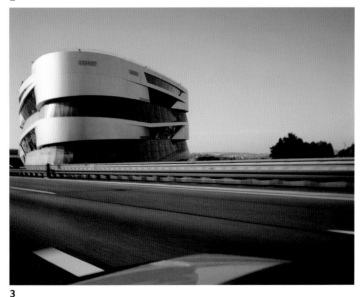

3

4

5

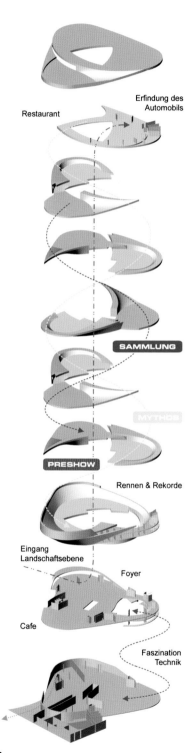

Erfindung des
Automobils

Restaurant

SAMMLUNG

MYTHOS

PRESHOW

Rennen & Rekorde

Eingang
Landschaftsebene

Foyer

Cafe

Faszination
Technik

6

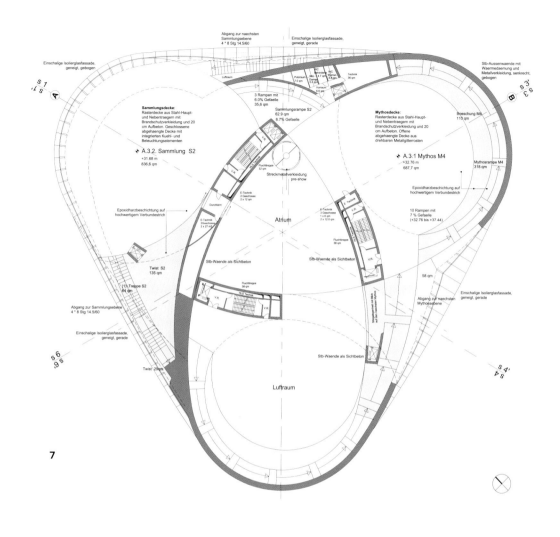

7

2 *Section rendering shows the interior display areas radiating around the high central atrium*   3 *The museum as seen from the nearby highway entering Stuttgart*   4 *The irregular surfaces of the museum convey an impression of movement*   5 *Display areas and ramps inside the main atrium*   6 *A layered presentation of interior spaces shows the overlapping display patterns that explain the history of the brand*   7 *The overall plan is very similar in form to the human heart, shows the atrium at its centre*

9

11

Opposite *Another view of the museum from the neighbouring highway, with its large external terraces* **9** *Light and shadow are orchestrated to highlight the automobiles on display* **10** *A stairway takes on an almost organic appearance; spaces throughout the structure are varied and unexpected* **11** *The powerful concrete forms of the structure form a backdrop for a long escalator* **12** *Views through the atrium are a highlight of the architectural spaces, with cars visible from almost every angle*

10

12

13 *Different routes through the museum are possible, with parts of the history of Mercedes concentrated in each section* **Opposite** *The evolution of the various types of vehicles created by Mercedes culminates in rooms such as this one with its views of the neighbouring countryside*

13

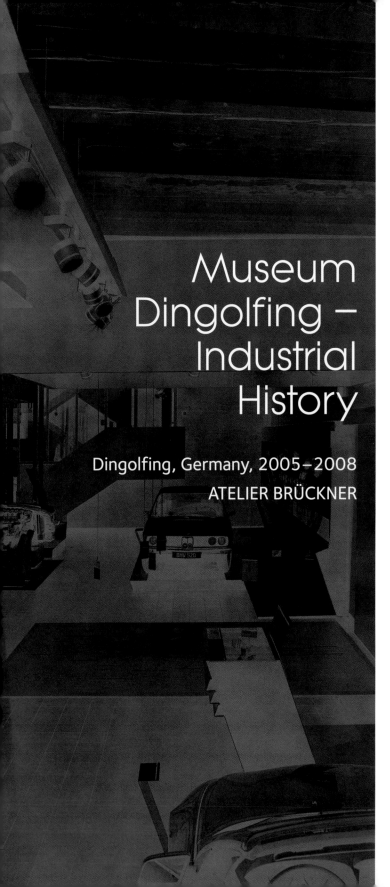

Museum Dingolfing – Industrial History

Dingolfing, Germany, 2005–2008
ATELIER BRÜCKNER

Dingolfing, in Southern Bavaria, Germany, is home to the largest BMW plant, but also, originally, to the Goggomobil, a micro car and motor scooter produced in Dingolfing after the Second World War by Hans Glas. The Glas Auto Works in Dingolfing was taken over by BMW in 1966.

Stuttgart firm ATELIER BRÜCKNER was commissioned to design the permanent exhibition of the Museum Dingolfing, which was inaugurated in November 2008. Approximately 1500 objects and artifacts concerning the Goggomobil and cars such as the BMW Z8 were installed in a chronological presentation in a former late-Medieval granary. The beginning of the industrial history of Dingolfing is presented on the second level, and exhibits on the Glas factory and the current BMW factory are on the middle and ground levels respectively.

The architects developed an exhibition system specifically tailored to this historic building and also to the industrial history of the town. Colour-coded and clearly divided according to periods, with an emphasis on the Goggomobil's influence on the 1950s street scene in Germany, this automotive museum is both original and highly successful.

1 *The display space of the museum is straightforward, with its emphasis on BMW cars as well as the original Dingolfing vehicles*

1

2

3

4

5

2 *A pump recalls the early history of the brand* **3** *Car parts and elements from Dingolfing production are juxtaposed on successive shelves* **4** *The early industrial history of Dingolfing is shown on the uppermost level of the former granary* **5** *A view from the opposite end of the upper level gallery* **6** *The Glas Automobile history is on the middle level* **7** *Close inspection of the vehicles by visitors is possible* **8** *Documents and photos accompany the cars on display*

6

7

8

10

9 *A car is shown separated from its chassis so that the structure is visible*   10 *Maps show the distribution of vehicles manufactured in Dingolfing*   11 *The presentation is didactic and straightforward, as is the documentation accompanying the exhibits*

11

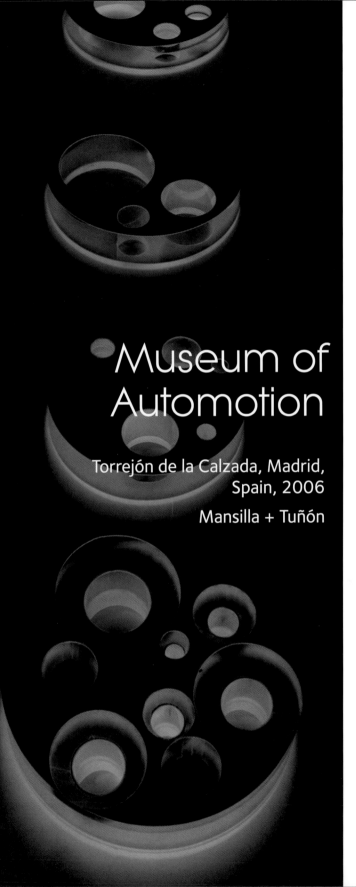

Museum of Automotion

Torrejón de la Calzada, Madrid, Spain, 2006

Mansilla + Tuñón

Situated between two highways, this remarkable structure makes reference to the history of Spain and its architecture, but also to the very material of the automobile. The architects state, 'Far from superfluous or secondary, the nature of this property is a reminder of the origins of the area and of how city outskirts have evolved and changed. Such developments, the outcome of industrial and post-industrial growth, owe their viability to one of its most prominent offspring: the automobile'.

The 30,000-square-metre structure is set on a site twice its size, which is divided by a stream. The museum is situated on the northernmost half of the lot. Circular in form, the design is intended to be evocative of Roman circuses and coliseums, as well as the castles and towers of the Castilian Middle Ages. Given its location, the museum is naturally closed to the outside environment like the historical fortifications the architects cited as a source. The sheet metal of the exterior frame is derived from recycled car bodies. Cylindrical light wells repeat the round form of the architecture.

As for the exhibition space, the architects explain, 'The exhibit area is the outcome of volumetric perforation based on a simple system of homothetic repetition of the overall cylinder; on the one hand, due to the large scale of the shell, this generates a single space for uninterrupted transit, a concatenation of smaller areas connected by the interstices between cylindrical light wells. And on the other, it establishes a visual cross-connection among the different strata of the building through the glass cylinders that pierce it'.

1 *With its recycled sheet metal exterior, the museum is situated, logically, between two highways* **2** *The exterior cladding of compressed automobiles is reminiscent of the work of the late French sculptor César*

1

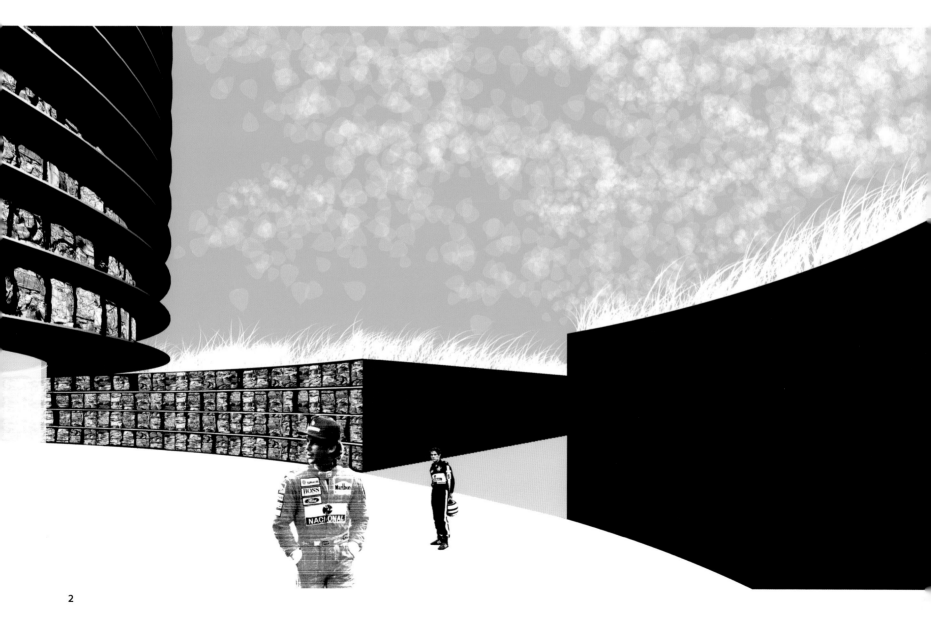

2

141

5

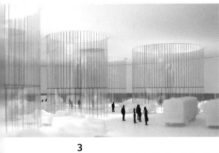

3

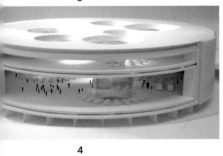

4

6

3 A circular motif is repeated in the museum interiors
4 The overall round form of the museum is visible in this model view where circular skylights can also be seen
5 Car bodies form the interior periphery of the museum walls as seen in this rendering **6** Cylindrical openings characterise the interior space and allow views from one level to the next **7** As this drawing of the entire structure shows, the design consists of a repetitive orchestration of round forms **8** A rendering emphasises the column-free simplicity of the space with overhead light coming through the round openings

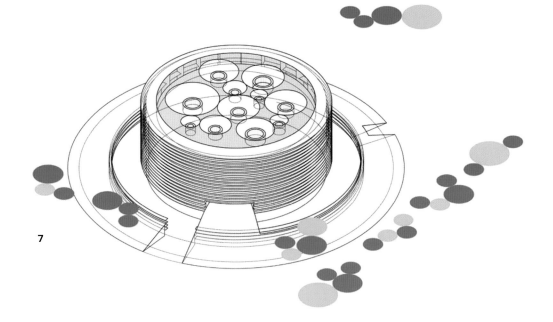

7

8

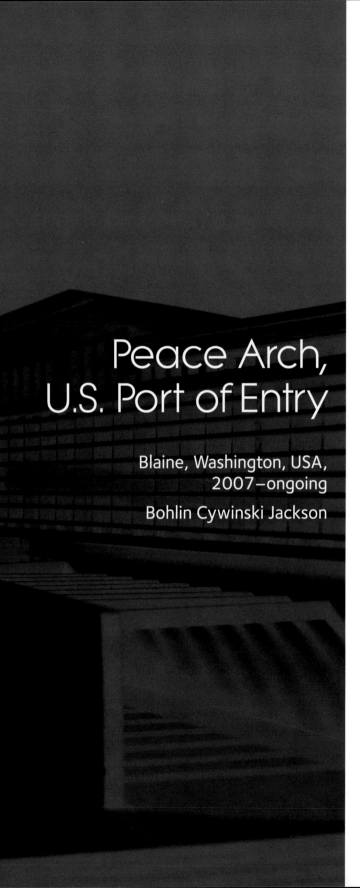

Peace Arch, U.S. Port of Entry

Blaine, Washington, USA, 2007–ongoing

Bohlin Cywinski Jackson

This building will stretch across the highway connecting Seattle, Washington, and Vancouver, Canada. Integrated into the existing Peace Arch State Park, the design provides 8200 square metres of new construction, including a 3200-square-metre port building with 10 lanes of inbound primary inspection, 40 spaces of inbound secondary inspection and a new highway bridge. The architects have in a sense embodied the land border between the two countries to create a facility that is as discreet in spite of its large and heterogeneous program.

The orientation and form of the building echo not only the border, but also the street layout of the city of Blaine and neighbouring agricultural windbreaks. The large secondary inspection facility has the same grid organisation as the more visible structure, but has an organic form, planted with native grasses to preserve the landscaped area. By careful site composition and minimising the visible size of built elements, the design accommodates expanded operational goals with limited disturbance to the surrounding landscape, preserving the character of this scenic roadway. Within its unique setting, the new Peace Arch U.S. Port of Entry creates a bold new vehicular gateway to the nation.

1 *Horizontal plates and volumetric detailing emphasise the long, low forms of the structures*

1

2

2 *A rendering showing the low, linear architecture* 3 *A model view showing the structure nestling into its location with some spaces below grade open to the sky* 4 *A covered walkway within the building complex* 5 *Overall site plan, showing the US–Canadian border* 6 *The Peace Arch as viewed from Semiahmoo*

3

4

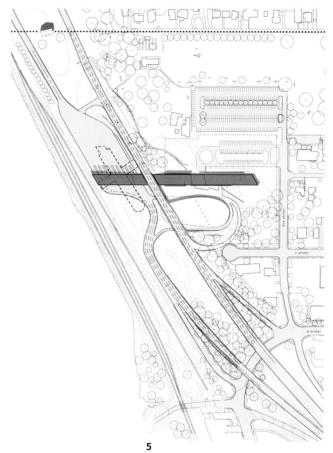

5

6

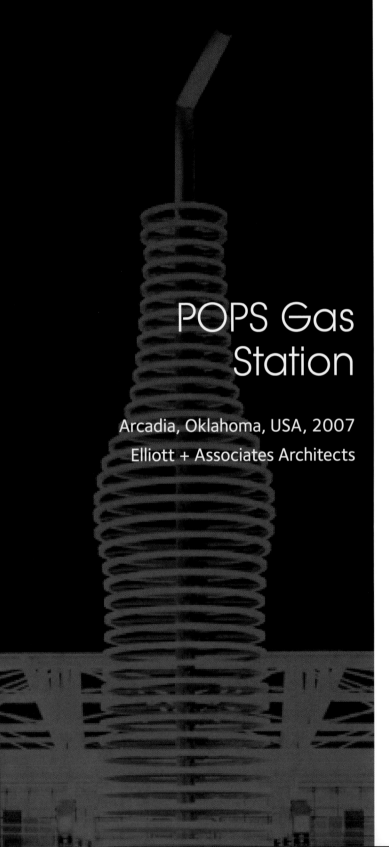

POPS Gas
Station

Arcadia, Oklahoma, USA, 2007

Elliott + Associates Architects

Located on the legendary Route 66, the POPS Gas Station is designed to portray the image of freedom on the open road. The structure, described by the architects as a 'roadside attraction', has a footprint of 510 square metres.

The architecture features a cantilevered canopy that runs unsupported over 33.5 metres. Covering the petrol pumps and allowing clients to enter the station without getting wet in the rain, this great metal canopy defines the structure more than any other feature including the giant, illuminated soda bottle with a straw that stands in front of the pumps. The designers refer to the great steel bridges and derricks all along Route 66 as a source of inspiration. As they say, POPS has a wood floor, historic photos of Route 66 and 12,000 pop bottles in the window in every imaginable colour. Red neon adds a glow and defines the cash register.

Service stations and roadside buildings have a long and often quirky history in the US. POPS redefines this tradition, allowing architecture and design to make an unexpected appearance in the middle of the country.

Opposite *The most striking feature of the architecture is this long sharply cantilevered canopy that covers the pumps* **Following pages** *The pumps are fully protected beneath the vast, column-free canopy*

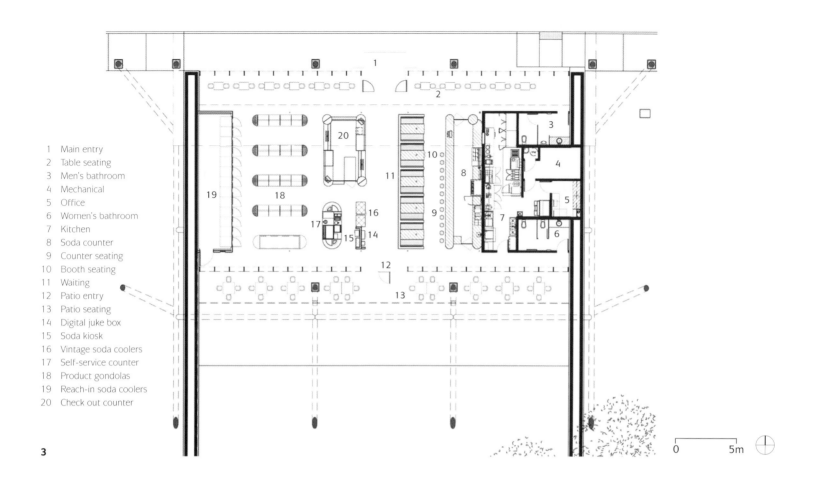

1 Main entry
2 Table seating
3 Men's bathroom
4 Mechanical
5 Office
6 Women's bathroom
7 Kitchen
8 Soda counter
9 Counter seating
10 Booth seating
11 Waiting
12 Patio entry
13 Patio seating
14 Digital juke box
15 Soda kiosk
16 Vintage soda coolers
17 Self-service counter
18 Product gondolas
19 Reach-in soda coolers
20 Check out counter

3

0   5m

4

5

6

3 *Store plan*   **4** *Seen from the side, the building looks almost as though it is only a canopy*   **5** *A large soda bottle feature with neon lights marks the front of the station*   **6** *Inside the station, a tilted wall displays carefully aligned soda bottles*

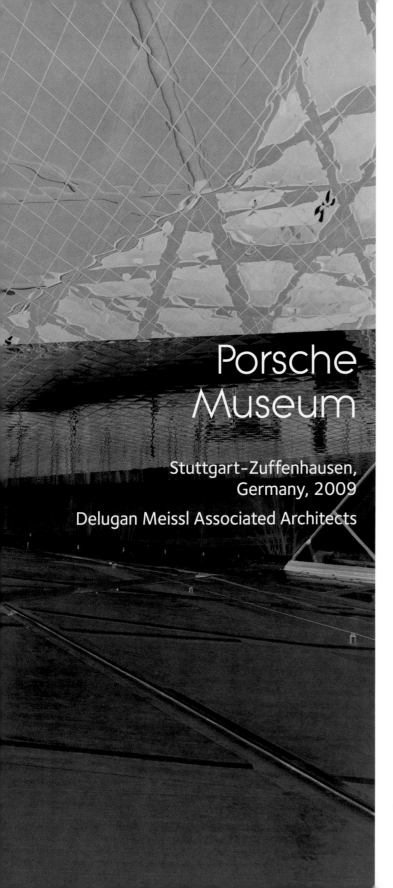

Porsche Museum

Stuttgart-Zuffenhausen,
Germany, 2009
Delugan Meissl Associated Architects

This 28,000-square-metre museum is expected to attract 200,000 or more visitors each year. The architects' concept was 'the translation of the versatile and vivid brand into the language of architecture'. The rather challenging site, near railway tracks and roads, seems to have inspired the architects rather than discouraged them.

Dynamically formed and monolithic, although its base and exhibition areas are intentionally 'decoupled', the museum is entered through a foyer flanked by a restaurant and a museum shop. A basic spiral pattern guides visitors into and through the exhibition zones. The building is to a large extent based on poured-in-place concrete with three-dimensional steel lattice formwork holding up a 'floating' superstructure. This mast rests on just three pylons with a 60-metre span between these load-bearing cores.

1 *The massive tilted form of the museum brings to mind a fast vehicle leaning into a sharp curve*

1

Opposite *Porsche motors can be seen on display in this view of the museum's exterior* **3** *The spectacular forms of the building as seen from a distance and an elevated angle* **4** *At ground level, the architecture's raked angles give an impression of continuous movement* **5** *At night, the museum glows from within, its surprising angles and volumes drawing the attention of visitors*

3

4

5

6

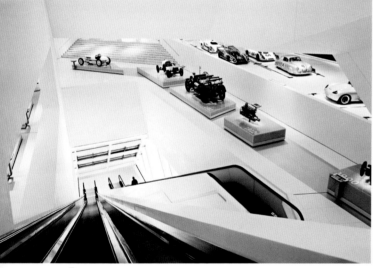

7

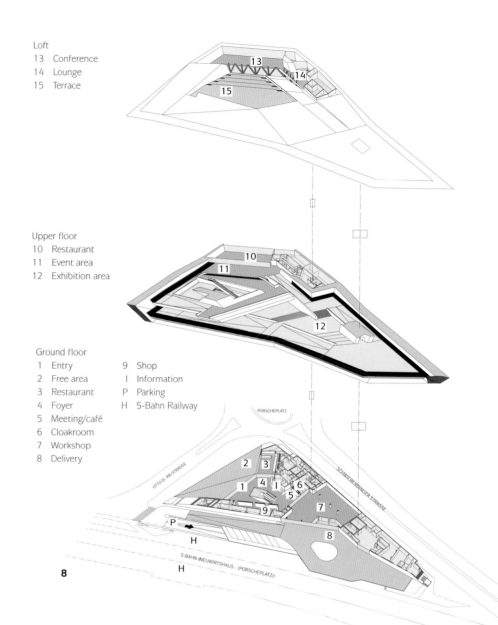

Loft
13 Conference
14 Lounge
15 Terrace

Upper floor
10 Restaurant
11 Event area
12 Exhibition area

Ground floor
1	Entry	9	Shop
2	Free area	I	Information
3	Restaurant	P	Parking
4	Foyer	H	S-Bahn Railway
5	Meeting/café		
6	Cloakroom		
7	Workshop		
8	Delivery		

8

6 *Inside the museum, clean lines and clear displays are the rule* **7** *Display area with escalators in the foreground and an emphasis on racecars and motors* **8** *Museum floor plan, showing train (S-Bahn) connection* **9** *Dark windows and the long escalator are sharply delineated against the whiteness of the interior*

9

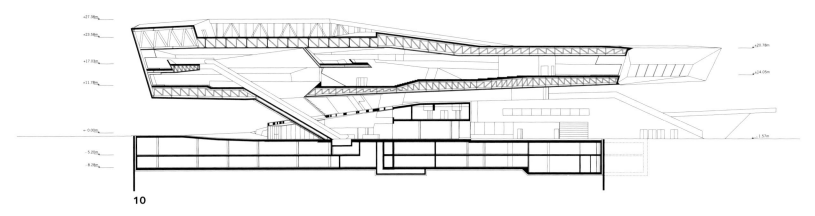

10

11

10 *Section showing the forward-leaning form and cantilevered volumes* **11** *Cars are displayed almost as if they were aligned on a racetrack* **12** *Seen from a distance, in the vast spaces of the museum, cars are presented like precious objects* **13** *Different vehicle types are grouped together – here the 917 series* **14** *The wrapping, curving forms of the architecture and interior spaces reveal the cars from unexpected angles* **15** *Road-hugging race vehicles seen from an appropriately low angle*

12

13

14

15

Project House, BMW Research and Innovation Centre

Munich, Germany, 2001–2004

Henn Architekten

The BMW Group's Research and Innovation Centre is located on a 33-hectare campus in Munich. The 90,000-square-metre Project House is located within the Research and Innovation Centre and seeks to open up new types of cooperation in the product development process as a result of its spatial organisation.

A studio workshop building is located in the central atrium of the 100-square-metre larger structure – conceived as a building within a building. Models representing different project stages are displayed on various levels, where they can be seen directly from the neighbouring project areas. This allows two new ways of communication: every designer can immediately switch between the virtual image on their virtual design screen and the real model.

The four project areas of the new Project House each consist of four quadrants; each quadrant comprises between 70 and 120 individual workstations. Levels are linked in pairs by spiral staircases, allowing an entire project team to work within the same spatial continuum.

1 *The building's broadly glazed areas glowing from within at night* **2** *Interior spaces viewed from above through the glass canopy* **3** *View from beneath the large glass canopy*

1

2

3

5

6

4 *The broadly curving interior atrium with views to offices and central meeting rooms* **5** *Two office levels linked by a spiral staircase* **6** *The double-skin façade in use* **7** *Site plan showing the Project House in the context of the larger BMW complex*

7

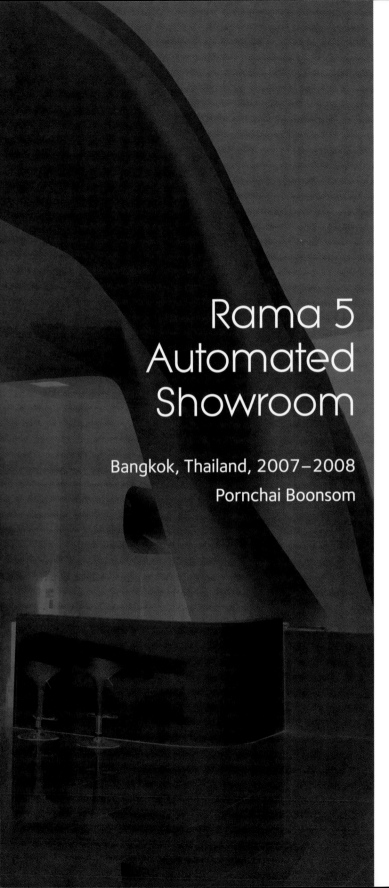

Rama 5 Automated Showroom

Bangkok, Thailand, 2007–2008

Pornchai Boonsom

The architect describes this automobile showroom as a 'yellow submarine-shaped building'. The 2000-square-metre structure was built on a new highway artery linking northwestern Bangkok to the city centre. The rapid movement of vehicles along this highway inspired the architect. 'The design', he states, 'was based on carrying information from one point of time to another with continuous motion relating interior space to the exterior of the building. The perceptual connection between the exterior and interior space is thus seamless'.

A yellow composite material is used for cladding, together with generous glazing, while the interior is completely white, attracting the attention of passersby. A sculptural stairway based on the curvature of the building links the first and second floors. An information counter is conceived as a flowing form linking the second and ground floors, while service, storage and support areas are located at the rear of the structure.

1 *The Ford logo appears discreetly against the strong curvature of an outside wall*

1

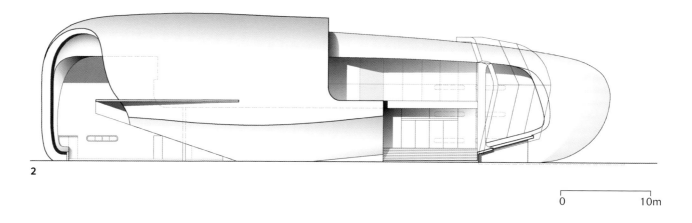

2

0   10m

3

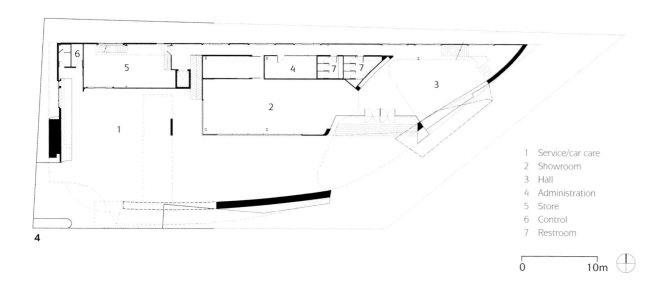

1 Service/car care
2 Showroom
3 Hall
4 Administration
5 Store
6 Control
7 Restroom

0   10m

2 *Elevation showing the building's shell-like form*   **3** *The structure in its urban context, seen from a similar angle as the elevation above*   **4** *Main floor plan*   **5** *Vehicles are wrapped in the broad curving forms that characterise both interior and exterior volumes*   **6** *Generous ceiling heights and an impression of movement in the architecture place the cars in their best light*   **7** *Furniture is nestled into the ample and unexpected interior folds of the architecture*

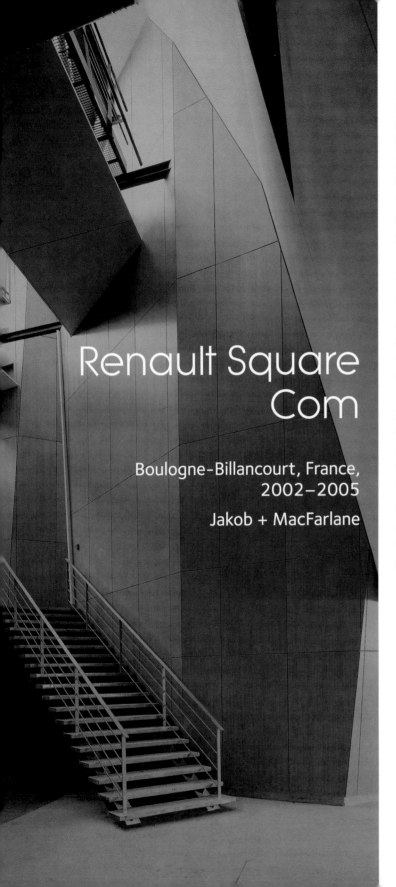

Renault Square Com

Boulogne-Billancourt, France,
2002–2005

Jakob + MacFarlane

Intended as a base for Renault's staff of about 250 public relations professionals and as a location to launch new cars and host seminars, Renault Square Com's history is linked to the firm's manufacturing facilities. The only example of 20 new manufacturing buildings designed by the French architect Claude Vasconi to be built in the early 1980s, this factory structure, called Métal 57m, was actually never used to build automobiles. The 15,000-square-metre building, with ceiling heights ranging from 6 to 12 metres, has the dimensions of a factory, but not necessarily those of a communications centre.

This was the challenge taken on by Paris architects Jakob + MacFarlane. They created three auditoriums seating 100, 300 and 500 people on one side of the building. On the other side they created a vast open exhibition area using exposed steel frames and 7-centimetre-thick structural honeycomb panels faced in resin-coated aluminium. As the architects explain, 'The wall material, made for aeronautics industry fuselages, is interesting because of its flatness and lightness'. The system's strength is such that automobiles can literally be hung from the walls. With its exterior form essentially unchanged, and such elements as heavy overhead cranes retained from the original design, this project is a careful and intelligent hybridisation of industry and communication.

1 *The basic building was built, as its form implies, as an automobile assembly plant*

1

2

3

2 *The architects took full advantage of the very high ceilings and industrial atmosphere of the original building* **3** *Sloping walls strong enough to carry suspended automobiles are aligned on either side of the main space*

4   5

4 *The walls added by the architects allow for the exhibition of automobiles both in the central space and in side auditoriums*   5 *The angled walls and display area added by the architects*   6 *The thin, suspended walls make the space look modern but do not eliminate its industrial character*   7 *The architects retained overhead cranes that can move vehicles inside the building*

6

7

9

10

11

Opposite *Despite the scale of the structure, the architects have succeeded in rendering the building thoroughly contemporary* **9** *Stairways and intermediate walls were added to allow for the creation of press conference auditoriums* **10** *While straight lines were the rule in the original building, the architects have added faceted angles* **11** *Views from almost any point emphasise the immense scale of the building*

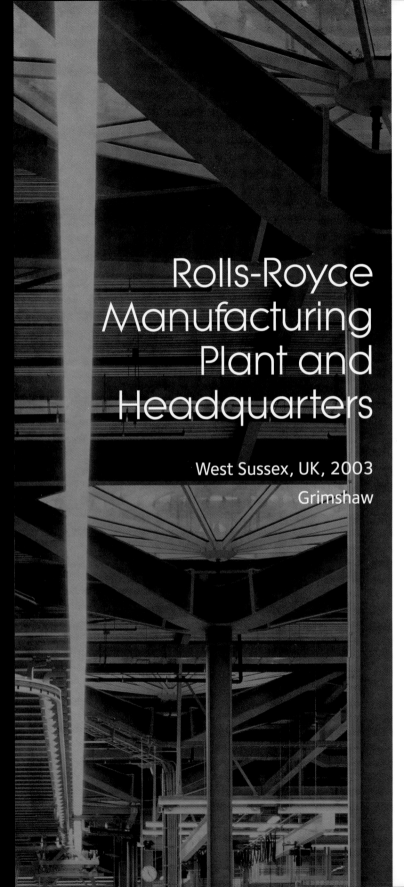

Rolls-Royce Manufacturing Plant and Headquarters

West Sussex, UK, 2003

Grimshaw

This 55,000-square-metre complex was built on a derelict industrial site in Goodwood, West Sussex, after detailed planning and environmental studies. It is a partially sunken design arranged around a central courtyard and surrounded by 400,000 new trees and shrubs. A green roof and Western red cedar cladding aid in blurring the distinction between the built and natural environments.

As the architects explain, 'The juxtaposed palette of industrial versus natural material forms a subtle expression of the Rolls-Royce ethos: the fine balance between technology and tradition, innovation and craftsmanship'. The complex includes a managerial and customer relations pavilion, a manufacturing plant and a paint shop. Visitor access is through the central courtyard and views into the production area are carefully composed.

The manufacturing building has a 20- by 20-metre grid design with steel 'tree' columns and 8-metre-diameter skylights. Wood and leather workshops and a viewing bridge are incorporated at mezzanine level in the high space of the plant. The two-storey pavilion structure is clad in glass, limestone and a curtain wall system with timber louvres. The restaurant, raised on angled pilotis, is set between the production and pavilion structures.

Opposite *This night view shows the uncommon transparency and lightness of the architecture*

2

3

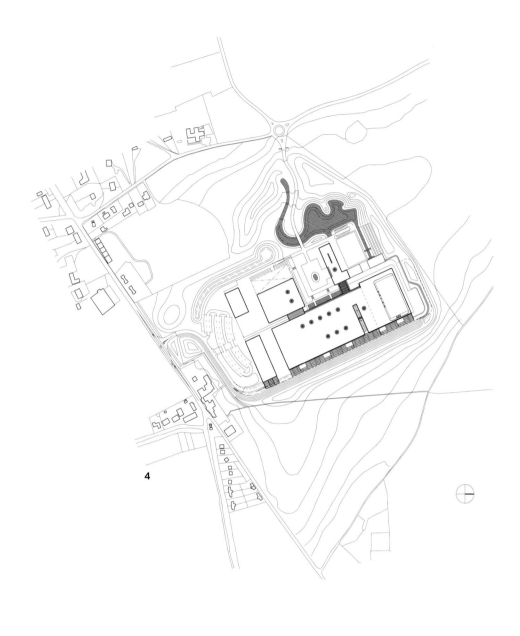

4

2 *Building section shows the vehicle assembly line*   3 *The building does not have the appearance of a traditional car assembly plant*

4 *Overall site plan showing a pond and the topographical lines of the site*

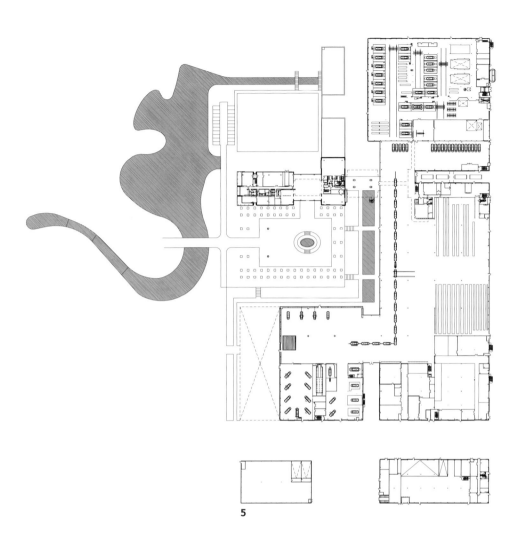

5

5 *Floor plan shows the rational and essentially rectilinear layout of the buildings* **Opposite** *The car assembly areas seem to fit perfectly into the architecture, which seamlessly blends the different functions required*

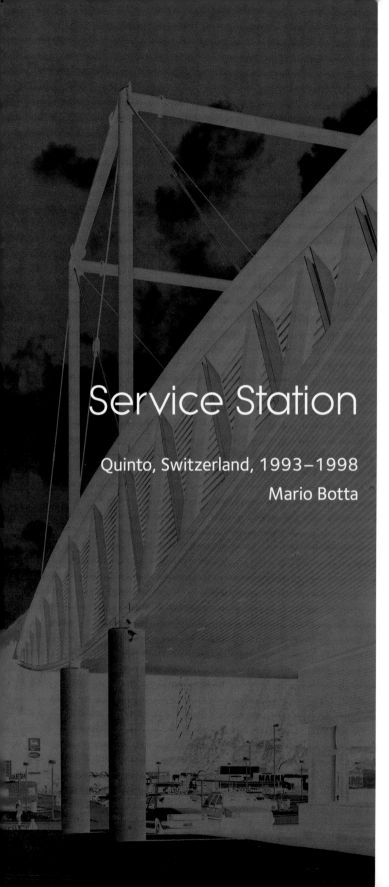

Service Station

Quinto, Switzerland, 1993–1998

Mario Botta

Mario Botta is best known for his private houses and chapels, but with this service station he took on a project on a very visible site near a highway. The winner of a 1993 design competition, this service station is located near the southern end of the San Gothard Tunnel in Quinto, Switzerland.

The basic 'airplane' wing design of the protective canopy above the pump areas and the station building are bright red enamel, making the structure stand out against both the highway and the mountainous natural environment. The 10.5-metre-high canopy measures 50 by 70 metres.

Set on a 46,500-square-metre site, the station covers 1130 square metres, and was built not for an oil company, but for the city of Quinto. Despite the iconic nature of service stations, it would seem that relatively few have been designed by architects as well known as Mario Botta. The result in Quinto remains a testimony to his talent for making even the most 'ordinary' structures eye-catching.

1 *Side elevation shows the actual service station building and canopy* **2** *A view of the pump area and overarching canopy with its rectangular support structure*

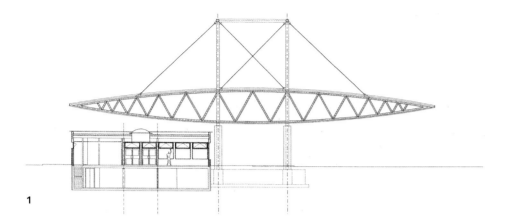

1

2

4

Opposite *With two simple cement support pillars, the canopy rises at the edges, conferring an impression of lightness* **4** *Seen from the side, the frame supporting the canopy is light, but its height also signals the presence of the station* **5** *On the highway side, the canopy and support frame allow clear views of the mountains of Ticino in the distance*

5

Shanghai Auto Museum, Auto Theme Park, Shanghai International Automobile City

Anting, Shanghai, China, 2006

ATELIER BRÜCKNER

The Shanghai Auto Museum is the first museum in China exclusively dedicated to the automobile and the history of its development. Opened in 2006, this 2400-square-metre facility focuses not on specific brands, but rather on topics centred on the concept of an abstract city. Road markings, like those in a city, define circulation patterns for visitors. The exhibition topics concern themes such as 'Exploration and Birth', 'Mass Production', 'Multiplicity and Diversity', 'Design for Speed', 'Sports and Driving' and 'Energy Saving and Compact Cars'.

ATELIER BRÜCKNER was responsible for the general planning, exhibition architecture and design and graphic design for the museum. The building's architect is IFB Dr. Brasch AG (Stuttgart).

A dynamic band of Corian forms the exhibition volume, defining the route and developing different spatial qualities. As a central design element it affords ease of orientation and leads the visitor through the history of the automobile, from its origins to the present. This timeline runs through the entire exhibition area and connects the themed 'topic rooms', taking museum visitors on a journey into the world of motion and speed.

1 *Floor plan shows the building's curving, almost amoeboid shape* **2** *Entry elevation highlights the building's long, folding lines and sweeping curves*

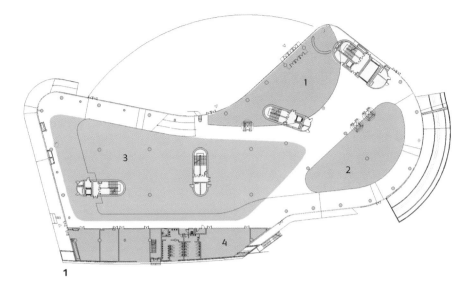

1 Foyer
2 Restaurant
3 Exhibition area
4 Service area

1

2

3

4

流线与速度
STREAMLINE AND SPEED

1960

5

6

7

8

9

3, 4 *Interior spaces are clean and well designed, in harmony with the exterior shapes of the building*

5 *Various vintage cars are placed in juxtaposition and explained with a timeline presentation*

6 *A Ferrari is presented at an angle, giving the illusion of motion*   **7** *Some of the earliest automobiles (an Oldsmobile on the right) are part of the display*   **8** *Cars are juxtaposed with explanatory panels*   **9** *Scale models and panels show the evolution of brands and car types*

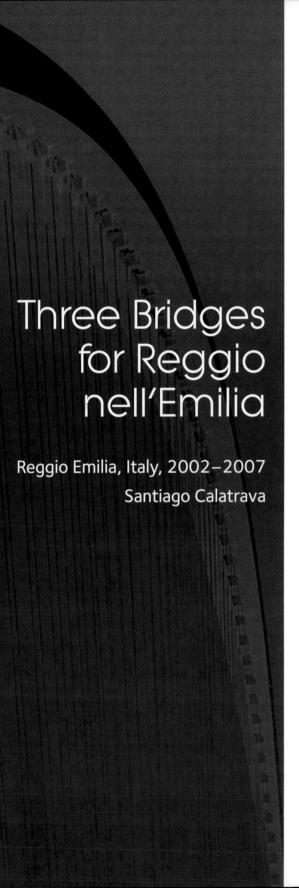

Three Bridges for Reggio nell'Emilia

Reggio Emilia, Italy, 2002–2007

Santiago Calatrava

Santiago Calatrava was called on to design a group of three bridges over the high-speed railway and A1 Motorway (Autostrada del Sole) in Reggio nell'Emilia, the capital of the northern Italian province of Reggio Emilia. The architect was also asked to design a new railway station (Stazione Mediopadana) on the Milan–Naples high-speed train line, as well as a comprehensive plan to create a dramatic new gateway to Reggio Emilia from the north.

This multiphase plan includes the three bridges, a highway toll station and other infrastructure to facilitate pedestrian, bicycle and automobile access to the city. Reggio nell'Emilia is located on a plain called the Padana and the architect felt that it needed vertical landmarks. He thus designed three very visible bridges, each made of reinforced concrete and white-painted steel, as the first phase of the larger project. The 46-metre-high central four-lane bridge, is 25.6 metres wide and spans 221 metres. It has a single symmetrical longitudinal arch and crosses over both the highway and the high-speed rail line.

The two other bridges are set at right angles to the flow of traffic and are placed to the south and north of the central element. With their total height of 68.8 metres, these two bridges are visible from a great distance. Cable-stayed and 179 metres long, they are 13.6 metres wide. A steel and glass toll station is located near the northernmost bridge. On the occasion of the inauguration of the bridges in 2007, Calatrava stated, 'I try to create bridges with a straightforward appearance that clearly belongs to the present. They use modern materials – concrete and steel – and are built with modern construction techniques. A modern bridge can also be a work of art, helping to shape not only the landscape but also the daily lives of the people who use it'.

Opposite *Santiago Calatrava sees these bridges as landmarks in the countryside, calling attention to vehicular traffic*

3

4

5

6

7

Opposite *The sweeping curves of these bridge arches give a decided impression of modernity to the roadway* **3** *Calatrava's skill as an architect and an engineer is evident in these structural solutions* **4** *A night view emphasises the lightness of a bridge and its arch* **5** *With its web of supporting cables, the bridge arch here resembles an oversized modern sculpture* **6** *Two bridge arches, turned at different angles and with different shapes* **7** *View showing the elegant disposition of the supporting cables and main bridge arch*

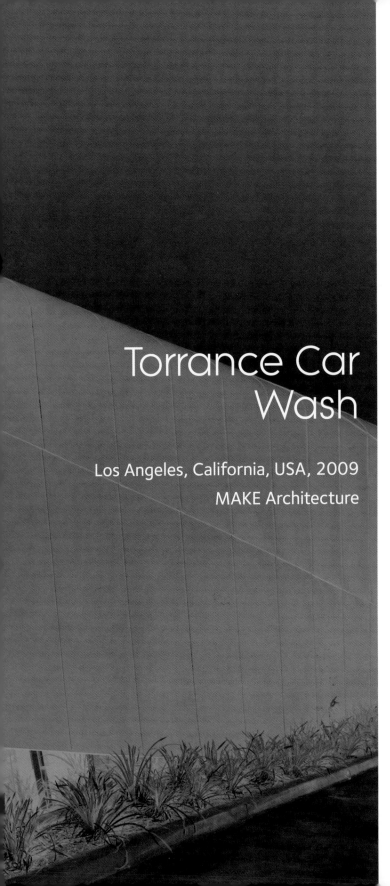

Torrance Car Wash

Los Angeles, California, USA, 2009

MAKE Architecture

Located on a 5880-square-metre site, this project includes an 854-square-metre retail building and a 302-square-metre car wash, both characterised by their folding metal panel designs. The architects explain that, 'California's car culture was traditionally supported by many iconic car washes located throughout the state. In recent years, the car wash has largely lost any sense of design let alone any iconic presence'.

When developing the Torrance Car Wash design, the architects' aim was to create a form that could be perceived as being in flux, to some extent evocative of the form of an unfinished vehicle design. The curves and folds of the car wash's skin reflect forms found in automobile design. The metal forms of the building fold up, 'visually moving alongside the cars as they pass'. To the south, ample glazing allows daylight into the car wash and allows onlookers to watch the machine as it works. The architects conclude, 'Instead of hiding the cars passing through the wash tunnel and the activity of the equipment, the glazing exposes these elements and makes the cars temporarily part of the life and design of the building'.

Opposite *The angled roof of the car wash clearly delineates the entry and exit*

2 *A simple folded roof and overhanging canopy signal the transparency of the facility* **3** *Plan showing parking spots, and the car wash zone, with the sequence marked with arrows* **4** *The architecture is both efficient and attractive*

2

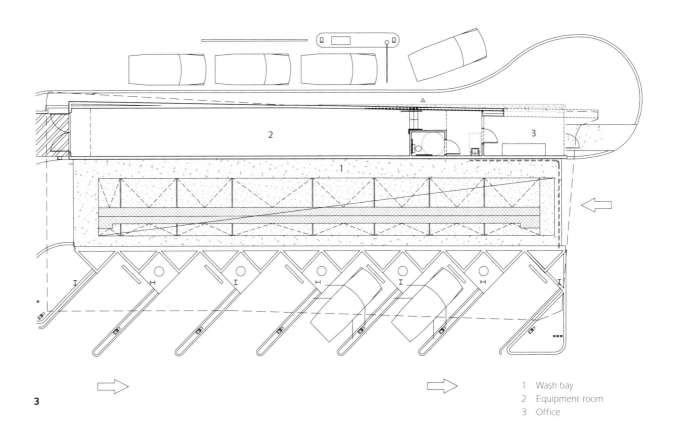

3

1   Wash bay
2   Equipment room
3   Office

4

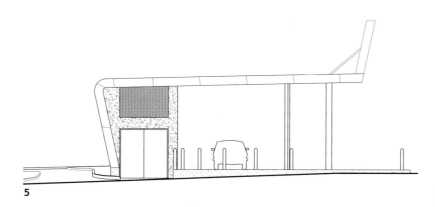

5

5 *An elevation showing the folded roof and the scale of cars within the space*   6 *The overall impression given by the architecture is one of lightness, as seen in the thin, tilted roof and the support columns*   **Opposite** *Detail of car wash exit*

6

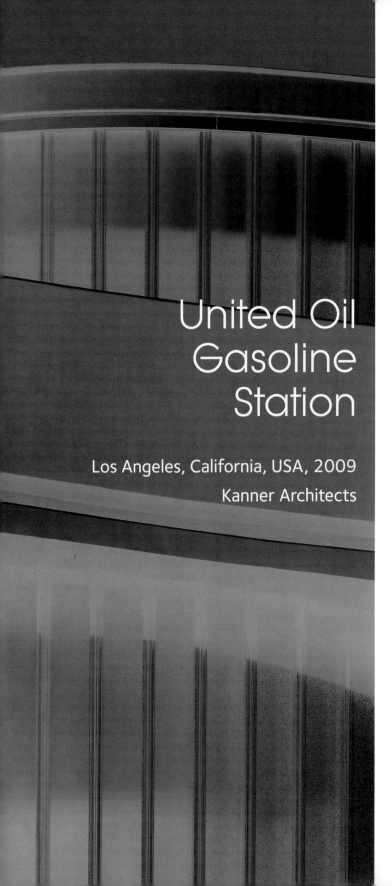

United Oil Gasoline Station

Los Angeles, California, USA, 2009

Kanner Architects

Located at the intersection of La Brea and Slauson Avenues in the Ladera Heights area of Los Angeles, the United Oil Gasoline Station seeks to reinterpret the most ubiquitous fixture of roadside culture – the service station. In a city where car and consumer cultures are so deeply entrenched in its inhabitants' collective psyche, how they 'read' and engage with the city is essentially via the windshields of their vehicles.

The design includes a 12-pump service station, a glass-box mini-market, a car wash and a pocket park located behind the store. Taking their cues from the infrastructural beauty of LA's concrete freeway interchanges, the designers have created a dramatic curving metal roof that rises to almost 11 metres above the pumps. An 8.5-metre-high oval channel-glass tower that encloses the 'cashier pod' within the convenience store recalls the large drum-like oil storage tanks located in the rugged hills nearby. The architects have also taken into account the presence of a large number of billboards, and imagined the entire United Oil Gasoline Station as a kind of architectural sign in itself.

Opposite *A dusk view emphasises the spectacular sweep of the canopy covering the pumps and the translucent station building*

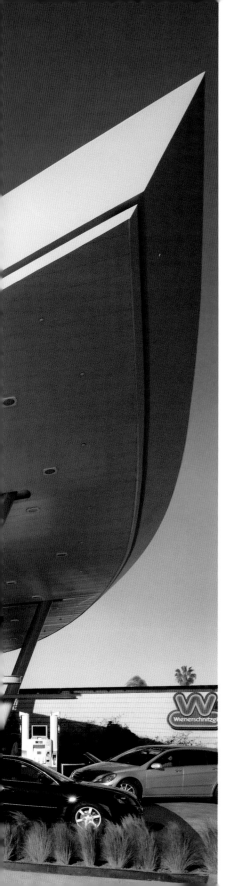

3

4

4 *A tilted canopy support column stands next to a pump and points the way to the station building itself*

Opposite *A night view showing the simple design of the pump spaces, less cluttered than typical gas stations*

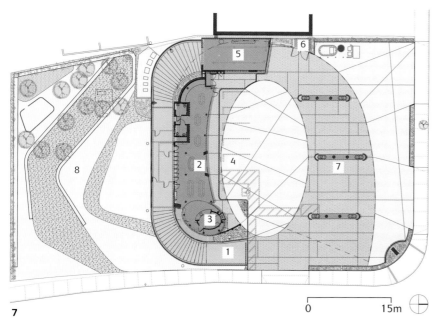

7

1 Ramp to car wash
2 Convenience store
3 Cashier
4 Parking area
5 Car wash
6 Garbage storage
7 Fuel pumps
8 Pocket park

0   15m

8

Previous pages *A column indicates the United Oil brand, and bright lights set into the canopy illuminate the pump area* **7** *Site plan showing the curvilinear forms of the station with its clearly delineated functions* **8** *Full-height glazing contributes to the overall impression of lightness in the architecture* **Opposite** *Seen from the exterior, the mini-market is fully visible because of the full-height glazing and bright lighting*

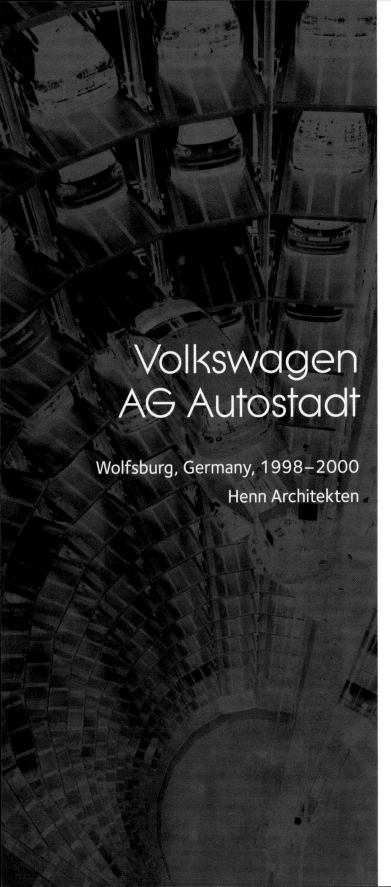

Volkswagen AG Autostadt

Wolfsburg, Germany, 1998–2000

Henn Architekten

This ambitious program is on 22 hectares in the corporate town of Wolfsburg, Germany. Working with landscape architects WES & Partner, Hamburg, Henn Architekten placed the complex in its own district with large buildings and pavilions, bridges, seas, tongues of land, hills, green areas, market squares and roads. Narrow and wide elements create a vivacious city image. With connections to the city, the railway station and the canal, the Volkswagen works and Wolfsburg Castle, the Autostadt Wolfsburg presents itself in the best location.

The complex includes the 2219-square-metre Audi Pavilion (1998–2000, in cooperation with Confino, Lussan), with a plan derived from the interlocking rings of the firm's logo; the 20-storey, 25,170-square-metre AutoTürme (1998–2000), which stores about 400 vehicles awaiting delivery; and the VW Pavilion (1998–2000, in cooperation with Furneaux Stewart, London and Grüntuch/Ernst, Berlin), which is described by the architects as 'a glass cube enveloping a sphere: a symbol of absolute perfection'.

1

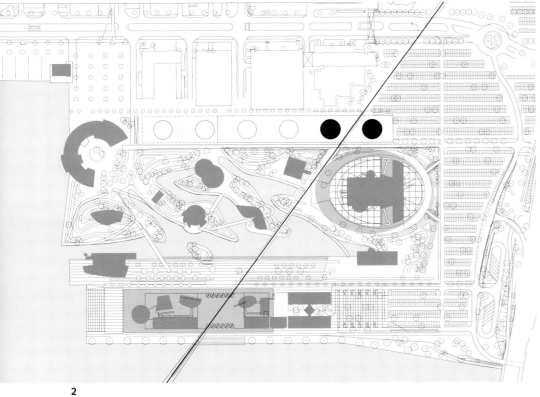

1 Overall view of the Volkswagen Autostadt campus   2 Site plan
3 The architects use a variety of modern forms such as cylindrical
towers and the floating cable-stayed roof seen on the customer service
centre   4 One of the automobile silo towers (AutoTürme) with its
extremely simple forms and lines; each tower holds 400 vehicles

2

3

4

213

5

6

214

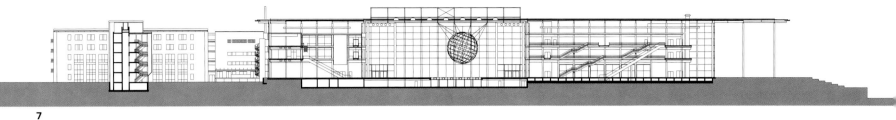

7

5 *A night view showing the Volkswagen Pavilion and the silo towers in the background* 6 *Aerial view of the Ritz-Carlton Hotel from within the Volkswagen Autostadt* 7 *Elevation of the 31,000-square-metre KonzernForum building* 8 *The edge of the KonzernForum, with the ZeitHaus building in the centre* 9 *Interior view of one of the automobile silo towers (AutoTürme)*

8

9

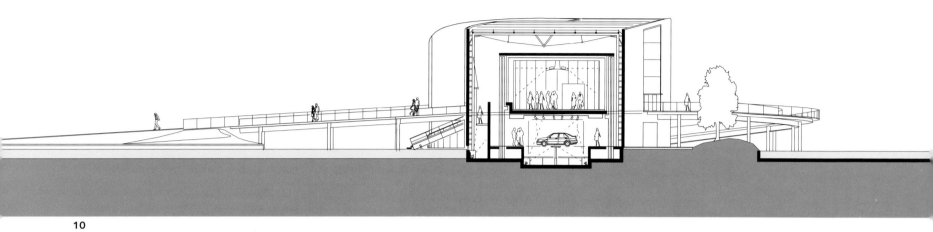

10

11

10 *Section of the SEAT Pavilion* **11** *The SEAT Pavilion as seen from its approach bridge* **12** *The Bentley Pavilion is described by the architects as being 'embedded in a hill like a jewel'* **13** *The Lamborghini Pavilion in its landscaped setting* **14** *The Audi Pavilion with the automobile silo towers to the left*

12

13

14

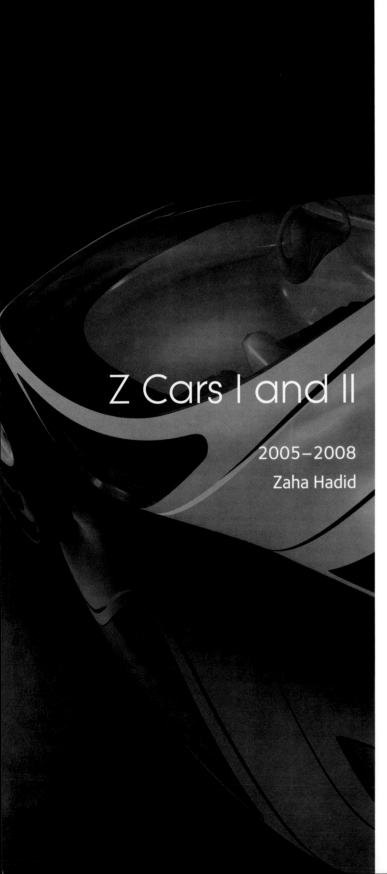

Z Cars I and II

2005–2008
Zaha Hadid

Frank Lloyd Wright, Le Corbusier, Walter Gropius and Buckminster Fuller all designed automobiles, thus the venture of renowned architect Zaha Hadid into this domain is not really a surprise. Hadid has demonstrated an abiding interest in overall integrated forms of design, including furniture, architecture and urban planning. The automobile, the manufactured object par excellence, may not be the easiest target for a designer who has shown a flair for unique, non-repetitive forms, where straight lines are the exception rather than the rule.

These concept cars were designed for well-known New York art dealer Kenny Schachter. The cars are battery powered and have innovative individual motors near their wheels. The flowing 'seamless' shapes fit in well with the aesthetics of Hadid's architecture and design, making clear her ambition to redesign just about everything, even things that move.

Opposite *Z Car I: Zaha Hadid applied her considerable design talents to creating a car that resembles her architecture*

3

4 Seen from various angles, the Z Car II is quite different from any other vehicle on the roads
5 A lower, side image emphasises the sporty aspect of the Z Car II
6 Seen from the rear, the Z Car II is also radical in its flowing simplicity   **7** As seen from above, the overall lines of the Z Car II are symmetrical, despite the irregularity of the windshields

4

5

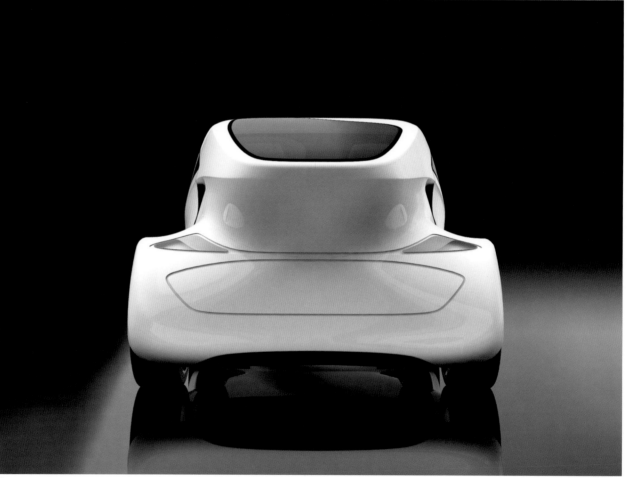

6

Image Credits

BMW Museum

Pages 60–61	Marcus Meyer
Page 62 (left)	Marcus Meyer
Page 62 (top, centre and bottom right)	ATELIER BRÜCKNER
Page 63	ATELIER BRÜCKNER
Pages 64–65	Marcus Meyer
Page 66	ATELIER BRÜCKNER
Page 67	Marcus Meyer

BMW Welt

Pages 68–70	© Ari Marcopoulos
Page 71 (top)	© COOP HIMMELB(L)AU
Page 71 (bottom)	© Hélène Binet
Page 72 (top left and right)	© Ari Marcopoulos
Page 72 (bottom)	© COOP HIMMELB(L)AU
Pages 73–74	© Ari Marcopoulos
Page 75 (bottom left and right)	© Ari Marcopoulos
Page 75 (top)	© COOP HIMMELB(L)AU

Citroën Flagship Showroom

Page 76–77	Philippe Ruault
Page 78	Manuelle Gautrand
Pages 79–81	Philippe Ruault
Page 82 (top)	Manuelle Gautrand
Page 82 (bottom left and right)	Philippe Ruault
Page 83 (left)	Jimmy Cohrssen
Page 83 (top and bottom right)	Philippe Ruault

Dubai Autodrome

Pages 84–89	Hufton + Crow

Ferrari Research Center

Page 90 (left)	© Maurizio Marcato
Page 90 (right)	Massimiliano Fuksas
Pages 91–92	© Maurizio Marcato
Page 93 (top)	Massimiliano Fuksas
Page 93 (centre)	© Maurizio Marcato
Page 93 (bottom)	Ramon Prat
Page 94 (top)	Ramon Prat
Page 94 (bottom)	© Maurizio Marcato
Pages 95–96	© Maurizio Marcato
Page 97 (top left and right, bottom left)	© Maurizio Marcato
Page 97 (bottom right)	Massimiliano Fuksas

Helios House

Pages 98–100	Eric Staudenmaier
Page 101 (top)	Office dA

Hessing Cockpit and Acoustic Barrier

Page 101 (bottom)	Eric Staudenmaier
Page 102	Office dA
Pages 103–105	Eric Staudenmaier

Hessing Cockpit and Acoustic Barrier

Page 106 (left)	ONL [Oosterhuis_Lénárd]
Page 106 (right)	Meijers Staalbouw
Pages 107–111	ONL [Oosterhuis_Lénárd]

In-N-Out Burger Westwood

Pages 112–115	Mark Lohman
Page 116 (top)	Kanner Architects
Page 116 (bottom)	Mark Lohman
Page 117	Mark Lohman

I-Way

Pages 118–121	Cyrille Druart

Lingotto Factory Conversion

Page 122	© Berengo Gardin Gianni
Page 123 (top left)	© Studio Merlo, Merlo Fotografia.com
Page 123 (top right)	© Lingotto
Page 123 (bottom)	© Berengo Gardin Gianni
Pages 124–125	© Berengo Gardin Gianni

Mercedes Benz Museum

Page 126	Christian Richters
Page 127	Brigida González
Page 128 (top)	UNStudio
Page 128 (bottom left)	Brigida González
Page 128 (bottom centre)	Christian Richters
Page 128 (bottom right)	Brigida González
Page 129	UNStudio
Pages 130–133	Christian Richters

Museum Dingolfing – Industrial History

Pages 134–135	Johannes Seyerlein, Munich
Page 136 (top and bottom left)	Thomas Furthmayr, Unterschleißheim
Page 136 (top and bottom right)	Johannes Seyerlein, Munich
Pages 137–139	Johannes Seyerlein, Munich

Museum of Automotion

Pages 140–143	Mansilla + Tuñón

Peace Arch, U.S. Port of Entry

Pages 144–147	© Bohlin Cywinski Jackson

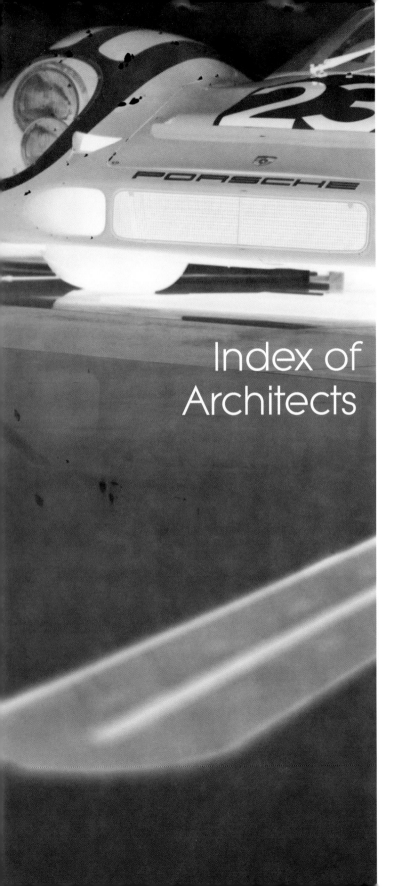

Index of
Architects